What people are saying about …

Kelly Minter's Books

The Fitting Room

"I believe Kelly Minter is one of the fresh voices God is using to reach our generation. I loved every word of *The Fitting Room* and wholeheartedly recommend its vulnerability, great teaching, and relevant life application. Kelly is a beautiful soul, and this book is a well-written reflection of God in her."

Angela Thomas, best-selling author and speaker

"Kelly has a marvelous blend of theological insight and girl-next-door likability. She's the kind of Bible teacher you'd also want to hang out with in a coffee shop!"

Lisa Harper, author and Women of Faith speaker

No Other gods

"I have loved Kelly Minter as a songwriter, worship leader, and wise teacher, but now I love her as an amazing author. *No Other gods* is fresh writing, biblical truth, and vulnerable, story-driven application. This book just became the next book I have to get for everyone."

Angela Thomas, best-selling author and speaker

"False gods. They're all around us, invading the crevices of our hearts and minds with such cunning maneuvers that we are often unaware of their presence. Thank the Lord for Kelly Minter.

Like a skilled lighting technician in a dark theater, she casts the spotlight of revelation right where it counts (and hurts)—into the recess of our souls—and she unapologetically exposes the reality of modern-day idol worship in all of us. This book, combining her personal journey and the power of Scripture, should be read by every believer who is ready to live fully and whole-heartedly for the one true God."

Priscilla Shirer, author and speaker

"With an engaging style and endearing vulnerability, Kelly Minter skillfully weaves timeless biblical truths together with practical, personal applications. Her words are sure to challenge and encourage many, no matter what their age or stage."

Jerusha Clark, author of *Every Thought Captive, Inside a Cutter's Mind,* and *The Life You Crave*

"In a time when Christian lives are becoming increasingly watered down, *No Other gods* reminds us of the one true God who is calling us into a relationship that is not only satisfying to our deepest longings, but also freeing to the secret parts of us that cry out for wholeness. This book inspires us to go to a depth of relationship with our Maker that is fresh and challenging."

Debbie Alsdorf, founder of Design4Living Ministries and author of *Deeper: Living in the Reality of God's Love*

"With our current society so focused on discovering the next 'idol,' we are easily drawn into believing we can find fulfillment in fame, money, or success. In *No Other gods,* we come face-to-face with our own 'small gods' that we believe can give us true satisfaction. Through Kelly's authenticity in her own journey, we are invited to take inventory of our hearts and urged to let go of idols keeping us from embracing the one true God."

Cindy West, director of Worship Arts, Woodmen
Valley Chapel, and author of *Saying Yes*

"In *No Other gods*, Kelly Minter has written a beautiful, personal account of a journey we all take from time to time that seductively leads us away from peace in pursuit of things that cannot satisfy. By drawing light onto the unseen and often overlooked impediments of her own, Kelly bravely leads the charge on the many areas we all share in common; and taking no prisoners along the way, she gently encourages us to wholeness by example. Fast paced, well written, honest and practical, *No Other gods* presents a bridge from where you are to where you could be. Great work."

Margaret Becker, songwriter and
award-winning recording artist

"Minter—worship leader, songwriter and author of the popular Living Room series of Bible study guides—offers readers surprising depth and breadth in this book on modern-day idols. It would have been easy to focus on surface idols such as materialism, beauty and media, and Minter does touch on those things, but she digs deeper into the false gods we really worship, using examples from the Bible throughout.... Minter does a fair amount of soul-searching, all with a healthy dose of humor that will have readers laughing while examining their hearts. Although it's marketed to women, this book will have a wide appeal to all Christian readers."

Publishers Weekly

The Fitting Room

The Fitting Room

Putting on the Character of Christ

Kelly Minter

transforming lives together

THE FITTING ROOM
Published by David C Cook
4050 Lee Vance View
Colorado Springs, CO 80918 U.S.A.

David C Cook Distribution Canada
55 Woodslee Avenue, Paris, Ontario, Canada N3L 3E5

David C Cook U.K., Kingsway Communications
Eastbourne, East Sussex BN23 6NT, England

The graphic circle C logo is a registered trademark of David C Cook.

The website addresses recommended throughout this book are offered as a
resource to you. These websites are not intended in any way to be or imply an
endorsement on the part of David C Cook, nor do we vouch for their content.

Unless otherwise noted, Scripture quotations are taken from the Holy Bible,
New International Version®, NIV®. Copyright © 1973, 1978, 1984 by Biblica,
Inc™. Used by permission of Zondervan. All rights reserved worldwide.
www.zondervan.com. Scripture quotations marked NASB are taken from the
New American Standard Bible, © Copyright 1960, 1995 by The Lockman
Foundation. Used by permission; KJV are taken from the King James Version
of the Bible. (Public Domain); and NKJV are taken from the New King James
Version. Copyright © 1982 by Thomas Nelson, Inc. Used by permission. All rights
reserved. The author has added italics to Scripture quotations for emphasis.

LCCN 2011920248
ISBN 978-1-4347-9985-2
eISBN 978-0-7814-0619-2

The Team: Don Pape, Karen Lee-Thorp, Amy Kiechlin,
Sarah Schultz, Jack Campbell, Karen Athen
Cover Illustration: Kim Thomas

Printed in the United States of America
First Edition 2011

6 7 8 9 10 11 12

060513

*To Maryn, Emmett, and Will, may you
always wear the clothes of Christ.*

Contents

Acknowledgments

I have been told that when you write a book, everyone close to you feels as though they are writing it as well. I think this is because the process of writing tends to be all-consuming. It works its way into conversation, demands focused attention, and requires special favors, such as, "Can someone make me dinner tonight, I need to write?" (I try to use that one sparingly). So, my deepest thanks to April, Mary Katharine, and Paige for "writing" with me. And to Lisa for being a steady and generous sounding board.

To my editor Karen Lee-Thorp, who plucked and rearranged at least a thousand stray words and helped me become a better writer. To all my friends at David C Cook, specifically Don Pape, Terry Behimer, and Jack Campbell, for giving me the shot at this manuscript and helping make it better.

The content of this book would not be without my mom and dad, who not only taught the virtues, but also lived them. There is no possible way to thank you except to live them back through the grace of Jesus. Megan, Katie, David, Brad, and Megen, I am incredibly blessed that each of you, my family, is known for your remarkable character.

Last, to all the incredible women I am blessed to speak to, write to, and serve, you are such a gift to me.

Where Are They When You Need Them?

The Virtues

A video shoot for a wonderful author and friend is taking place at my house this week. Stylists, cameramen, set designers, talent, and black-clad crew have been running around my home for days. The entire shebang has absolutely nothing to do with me except that twenty people are now using my bathroom. This is a girl's recurring nightmare. I've decided the only true payoff is the round-the-clock catering, which produces warm cookies every afternoon around three-ish—a routine I am trying to understand how I have lived so richly without.

This morning as the crew arrived, I feverishly applied the last few elements of makeup onto my slightly puffy and pillow-wrinkled face. I threw on my work-at-home uniform, which is made up of jeans, a

T-shirt, and socks if the hardwoods are chilled, flip-flops if it's summertime. As I meandered through the kitchen—for the catering, of course—I ran into a stylist I knew who was working with the talent. I told her I needed help finding new boots for the winter. She agreed at an alarming rate, well acquainted with my wanting shoe collection. Her exaggerated urgency was tongue-in-cheek, but with a hint of dead-serious. After all, she is a stylist. Clothes are what she does.

If ever there was a spell in history when what we wear is paramount, I daresay it is now. Dress is a multibillion-dollar industry. The garments we drape on our backs, the hats we don on our heads, the jewelry that dangles from our necks and wrists all tell a little of who we are. Our dress is an expression of ourselves, a statement of our personalities or moods. We dress up, we dress down, we dress for comfort, we kill ourselves in high heels to dress for style, we dress for the weather, we dress for others, we dress for ourselves. But what about the dress of our souls? What about the way our character clothes us? And our character *does* clothe us. We give off far more than we will ever know by the way we greet the barista, drive in traffic, enter a room, answer the phone, glare at our toddler who's having a meltdown in a non-meltdown-friendly environment. If only it were as simple as hiring a stylist for an extra bag of peace or another color of honesty. Could I get some denim patience for under $100?

I promise not to kill you with the clothing metaphor for the next several thousand words, but I want to pull from the comparison the apostle Paul set in motion in a letter to the Colossians: "Therefore, as God's chosen people, holy and dearly loved, *clothe* yourselves with compassion, kindness, humility, gentleness and patience" (3:12). A few verses earlier he writes, "You have *taken off* your old self with its practices and have *put on* the new self, which is being renewed in knowledge in the image of its Creator" (vv. 9–10). The image of clothing, the picture of slipping out of the old and sliding into the new, is an easily digestible concept because we dress every day.

The gap in the metaphor comes when we don't know how to clothe ourselves in Christ's character, or when we've given it our valiant best and come up short … *really* short—like we just walked out the door in our towel, and everyone is staring and mortified while we grasp for fig leaves from our ailing character-garden. The breakdown occurs when we were never taught the value of integrity, when anger and resentment were the prominent traits our parents passed down, when we weren't modeled the fine art of forgiveness, when sexual escapades were our solution for loneliness, when lying seemed to work better than the truth at untangling our predicaments, or when complaining became our default over contentment.

Basically, the spiritual concept of throwing off scratchy wool for designer silk sounds simply effortless, but the real-life version is another matter altogether. Many of us who have attempted such a wardrobe overhaul have come up frustrated rather than inspired, and this for many reasons we will address in the pages to come. I hope to speak to these struggles while looking at specific character qualities less from an academic view and more from the vantage point of our everyday realities. Because most of us know we're supposed to take off old things like bitterness and anger and full-on recklessness and put on the new self, which is full of qualities such as kindness and joy and self-control. But knowing this doesn't automatically make it so.

I can fairly easily write about what these new-life virtues are, their characteristics, and how we need more of them in our lives, but that feels just about as helpful as the book I was reading last night that appropriately told me not to eat out of boredom or past seven o'clock, which triggered the thought that I might be a little bored, which reminded me of the homemade cinnamon-raisin bread I had in the kitchen. Before I could be held responsible for my actions, I had lost my place in the book and was standing in my pajama pants eating bread.

See, I'm pretty sure most of us need more heart transformation than we need more head knowledge, whether it's about food or far more important things like exhibiting the character of Christ. Knowledge is vitally important, but it seems so many of us in Western Christianity are just crammed with it—really important knowledge that we gain in controlled settings like Bible study—but when up against the prospect of forgiving someone who has just ripped our insides out, or needing to grab patience out of thin air after our roommate has just stepped on our ever-loving last nerve, we are left with a ton of knowledge about what we *should* do (don't eat the bread when you're bored) but have no idea *how* to do it.

〰〰〰〰〰〰

I had the rare blessing of growing up with parents who modeled and taught the character of Christ well. They were big on the "how" of character and emphasized it over most everything else: A struggling grade on an algebra exam was more excusable than lying (which ended up working heavily in my favor … *coefficients?*); an off game on the basketball court was no problem compared to being disrespectful to a teacher. My parents taught my siblings and me at a young age about humility, gentleness, patience, contentment, gratefulness, purity, and so on. This doesn't mean I'm good at all these things; it just means I had the privilege of being taught them. And now that I am past most of my adolescent outbursts and full-on temper tantrums—so often directed toward my parents' instruction—I am ever thankful for their guidance. If only they could get paid back in stocks or something.

Still, the virtues revealed in Scripture are hard enough when you've been taught them. But what if you've never been exposed to them in the first place? Perhaps it is in response to this question that my deepest desire for the following pages is to shed fresh light on some of the seemingly shadowed and antiquated virtues in Scripture, exposing their beauty, their delicacy, and the freedom in which they are meant to tailor our lives. This is important because so many of us are plainly stuck in life, wearing the same old things and getting the same miserable results. Our character clothes are frumpy, because we've never been groomed and fitted from the pages of Scripture.

There are others who are all too aware of the characteristics of godliness but want nothing to do with them, because they were taught such virtues by people who didn't actually live by those principles. For them, the notion of godly character was flaunted by hypocrites, self-righteous leaders, or possibly angry parents, and they haven't wanted a piece of its polyester since. Yes, a lot of damage has been done in the name of God and Christian virtue; people have been clothed by reckless tailors. However, one of my greatest hopes is that if this has been your experience, you will give the discovery of authentic godliness another look, because biblical virtues are not punitive but life-giving.

If there are those who have had little exposure to what the Bible says about godly character and those who have had lots of exposure but find it legalistic and binding, then there is a third group as well: those who long to grasp hold of godly traits but find them maddeningly unattainable. Perhaps you have tried to wear godliness like you try to lose weight or work out or stick to a New Year's resolution. You've dug deep but have found that things like moral purity, kindness, or humility simply don't exist in your closet. You've worn the knock-off brands that faintly resemble the real thing, but after a few good washes of reality, their colors fade and their seams split. And so you find yourself not necessarily disdaining the virtues, but having given up on them.

This is a common dilemma, mostly because we mistakenly view godly character qualities as things we can accomplish if we try just a little harder. We promise ourselves we'll hold our tongues next time or be thankful for what we have. Perhaps one day we muse we'll graduate to stretching our reserve of patience, or we'll respect ourselves enough to stop sleeping with acquaintances. But we can never separate the qualities of God from God Himself. True Christian virtues are not something we can slap on ourselves like cutout clothes for paper dolls. They come as a result of heart change that is accomplished through the supernatural love of Jesus. And yes, we will expound on this more, because I am challenging myself not to offer Christian colloquialisms that are easy to throw out; even though some of them are true, most are vague and inaccessible.

I have experienced the frustrating failures of trying to "do better" as a Christian. I've been damaged by legalistic authorities whose preaching and practicing lived in entirely different zip codes. And

I've had times when I just didn't know much about the heart behind godly virtue, even though my parents gave me a great foundation. Still, the authentic changes that the gentle and unyielding characteristics of holiness have brought about—and are bringing about—in my life are wholly divine and transforming. Not to mention enormously practical.

Practical, because there are relationships that need to be healed from the cancer of bitterness. There are bones that need to be freed from the incessant gnaw of anger. Hurting neighbors who need to hear an encouraging word of kindness instead of the latest morsel of gossip. Children who need to know that we've been blessed in our Western society and that contentment is healthier than complaining. Husbands who need peaceful wives instead of anxious ones; wives who need comforting husbands instead of critical ones. Friends who need to be given to instead of demanded from.

⁓⁓⁓⁓⁓⁓⁓

I recently wrote a piece that included a list of several virtues, and I asked women to chime in on the virtues they found the most difficult. This was a bit of a trick question, because the virtues are probably all equally hard in their own right, but I was curious as to what their comments would include. I could not have been more delighted by one woman's sincere reply: "I think I have plenty of each when I don't need them. It is only when I am in the situation that I discover that the one I need is the one that I am short of." This is pure genius. I pondered her sentiments as a possible subtitle to this book: *Clothing Yourself in the Virtues You've Got Plenty of Until You Need Them.*

Of course the very essence of biblical virtues is that they're only virtues when they're being tested: Patience is not patience if someone or something is not trying it. Forgiveness is not forgiveness if there is no offense to pardon. Humility is not humility if a person never has to bow. Biblical virtues need to be studied and defined, but if we leave them in the Christian classroom, we will find we've got a wardrobe literally bursting with them until the moment we're invited to the ball.

If this is has been your experience as it has often been mine—if you find that you have virtues in droves until the moment you need them—it may help to go back to the beginning. To begin with God and what He has accomplished that enables us to live all the virtues He embodies. Much of this can be summed up in the opening line of Colossians 3:12: "Therefore, as God's chosen people, holy and dearly loved …" See, we can't really get to the virtues in Scripture until we have a good handle on the truth that we have been chosen, made holy, and are dearly loved. If we take this introductory line away, we are left with a list of dos (clothe yourselves with compassion, kindness, humility, gentleness, patience …) without any context for them.

Once we understand the context, the way is paved for the often-painful work of parting with our old wardrobes, even that A-outfit from college we're pretty sure we'd still look fabulous in. 'Cause the old and the new don't coalesce—our human natures don't meld with the character of Christ. But leaving the old behind can be surprisingly liberating, because it leaves us poised to wear the virtues we will explore in the pages ahead: forgiveness, peace, kindness, humility, compassion, and patience, with a sassy feather of joy in our hats. Virtues that won't mysteriously disappear when the clock strikes twelve, ones that will actually be there when we need them.

Pick Me, Pick Me
Chosen

"Therefore, as God's chosen people, holy and dearly loved, clothe yourselves …" There's an order to this whole virtue-clothing process. You can't bounce on the tip of the Colossians 3:12 diving board, spring over its first line, then cannonball into the sea of virtues with a splash. It doesn't work that way, unless you're into belly-flopped attempts at religiosity. And yet for many years this was my story, as I unknowingly sailed right over Paul's opening "Therefore," cutting straight to the bottom-line list of virtues. My mind-set was, *Just give me what I need to do, who I'm supposed to be*. Forgiving? I'll figure it out. Kindness? I think I can probably smile a little more. Patience? I'll consider blood-pressure medication.

You may not be like me in this way at all, but I grew up very duty bound. Part of this is in the Minter DNA. My late grandfather was the superintendent of the Naval Academy and commanded the *Intrepid*. My dad is the pastor of a distinguished church just outside of Washington, DC, a church he founded thirty-seven years ago. I have an aunt and uncle who left prominent lives in the navy to live in a hut in the middle of the jungles of Papua New Guinea to tell people about Jesus. My other aunt married a young navy man who is now a retired admiral, and she has traveled the world, entertaining and hosting as the quintessential military wife, serving her country tirelessly. One of my cousins is studying for six years in Rome to be a priest (after seven years on a nuclear submarine). Cobble all this together with a strict and intense Christian school upbringing, and you've got one uptight kid trying really, really hard to be successful at being good. Not to mention the added intensity of my basic personality—which manifested itself when I was four and my mom asked me if I would like to know Jesus as my Savior, to which I responded, "Not until I understand the whole Bible."

For me, duty usually came before grace and relationship. Instead of understanding that I was already chosen, made holy, and loved, I understood the virtues outlined in Scripture as prerequisites for God's favor, things I needed to try hard at so I *could* be chosen, holy, and loved. Without knowing it, I was trying to live up to the virtues so I could somehow obtain these blessings I already had in Christ, not the other way around. My thought process went something like *If I can have more humility, God might choose and bless me. If I can forgive more thoroughly, surely this will count for some additional holiness. And if I can just manage to be more compassionate and kind, God's love might find me more worthy.* But Colossians 3:12 turns all of this around. It's not "Therefore, since you are a compassionate, kind, and humble person, you now get to be holy, loved, and chosen by God." Instead, it's quite the opposite. Through Christ, we as believers are made holy *before* we are patient and loving. We are chosen *before* we are kind and forgiving. We are loved *before* we learn how to be gentle and compassionate. It's more like, since we are chosen, holy, and loved, we get to dress like what we already are.

I have a friend whose dad is very dear to me. He's eighty-six this year with scarcely a wrinkle. He keeps his white hair neatly combed and a close eye on his finely trimmed beard. He'd no more have a whisker out of place than a barnacle on his boat. He has blue eyes and olive skin, all his features working off one another like a finely decorated room. He was in the navy only five years before meeting his wife and moving on to a career with a phone company, but apart from the love of his life and his dynamic children, that brief stint in the navy bottled some of the most magical years of his existence.

You can't sit with him more than a couple minutes before, "Did I ever tell ya about that tour off the coast of Thailand?" Or, "When we were sweeping the mines in the Tsushima Straits ..." He could fill tomes with his stories, which is surprising for a relatively brief naval career. But I think he has so many stories because he absorbed and cherished every remarkable moment he spent in the glory of the navy. He had grown up poor and invisible, longing to be part of something that could offer him a grander and more meaningful life than the one he knew. He explains this in a story I have affectionately memorialized as the pencil story:

When he first enlisted in the navy, he was given a pencil. Of course, he had used pencils before in his writing and arithmetic classes, but none of them had actually been his. And up until that moment, he had only written with pieces of pencils, ones with shredded erasers, peeling yellow paint, and dull points. Until the navy he had never held a bright, smooth, still-wooden-scented *pencil*. It was given to him as part of the standard allotment to new enlistees. It was new, and it was his. And something about holding a brand-new pencil—his at the first jot—signaled he was part of something that would change his life forever. This story gets me every time; plus he tells it with an aged New York accent, so there's a fitting cadence and authority to it. Not surprising, the pencil story always leads to the uniform story, where he tells of receiving his first never-before-worn navy attire. He washed and ironed and kept his blue and gold garments like the gold was the real thing—though I think he'd argue that getting to wear the navy gold that's measured in prestige is more valuable than the kind that's weighed in karats.

The thing about the uniform that still tears him up almost seventy years later is not that he'd gotten a new suit, but that the suit meant he was part of the navy. The uniform didn't qualify him to be in the navy, but because he was in the navy, he got to wear the uniform. I think that's a little of the idea the apostle Paul's trying to get across in Colossians 3:12, that clothing ourselves in the virtues doesn't make God love us, but since God already *does* dearly love us, we get to wear the clothes of virtue. *Therefore,* as a navy sailor, wear your uniform because you're entitled to, and it tells everyone who you belong to and the great country you stand for. *Therefore,* as someone who has been made holy, who is chosen and loved, wear compassion, kindness, humility, patience, forgiveness, peace, and joy, because this, too, is the clothing you are entitled to wear since you are in Christ.

.vwwwwwwv

Since Paul begins Colossians 3:12 with the idea of God choosing us, I will start with the innate desire to be chosen. A longing that manifests itself early in life. I remember little more vulnerable and nerve-racking than being a kid out on some field or cul-de-sac, gearing up for a game of softball or kickball, anxiously waiting to be chosen by one of the team captains. It was important for your reputation and overall standing in the kid community to go early. A lot rode on your name being called at the top of the selection process, because every name before yours lessened your cool factor significantly. I wanted to be wanted, and given my sensitive nature, I wanted everyone else to be wanted too, but being chosen in this manner didn't really allow for such equally dispersed value.

None of these experiences, however, could prepare me for the rejection of my senior prom, which possibly topped my all-time list of least-chosenness. (*Least-chosenness* is not technically a word, but I'm pretty sure Webster peered down from heaven on my prom night and thought, *Whup, missed a word.*)

In high school I was part of a huge group of friends, and remarkably we all stuck together during those tumultuous and fickle years that tend to toss and scatter us around. We were almost perfectly split between boys and girls, so this played out nicely for dances and events, if not also for four years of guaranteed erratic emotions for the females. When prom rolled around, the couples who were already dating were shoe-ins for the dance, which left the rest of us to mostly pair up as friends. One by one, the guys asked the girls, and each day unveiled a simultaneous excitement and relief for whomever had newly secured her date to the most built-up night of our lives.

After every one of my girl friends had been asked, I realized there was only one boy left—let's call him Matt—who hadn't asked anyone to the dance. The days were expiring like sand slipping through an hourglass. Things were looking especially bleak, because I had also heard through the grapevine that Matt wasn't even planning on going to the prom, since he had broken up with his girlfriend of three years just a few months before. After pretty much losing my grip on the last of any diaphanous hope and talking myself into thinking that staying home with my parents and younger siblings that night would be *so* much more fun, I got the call. Matt's buddies had encouraged him not to miss out on the most coveted night of high school, whether he was still with his girlfriend Nina or not. (Now, Nina's name I cannot change, because you just can't change a name like *Nina*.)

I remember Matt's words pretty clearly: "Hey, Kelly." *Nervous high-school pause.* "Umm, so you know I wasn't going to go to the prom ..."

"Um, yeah, I think I heard that." *More nervous silence on both ends.*

"Well, I've been thinking that I don't want to miss out on this, like, really big night with all our friends ... and since you're, well ... the only one left not going, I thought, um, maybe we could go together."

Feeling super loved, chosen, and desired. "Yeah, I would love to."

"Great! Um, so I guess I'll see you tomorrow."

"Okay, yeah, at school. I'll be there."

More awkward banter until, hallelujah, this phone call was finally put out of its misery.

Phew! So I was going to prom! *Yes!*

I made all the necessary rounds of phone calls to my girl friends, met mostly with heightened screams and squeals: "We knew it would happen for you! We just *knew* it!" The next couple of weeks ensued with dress shopping and jewelry swapping, with lots of romantic dreams and discussions with one another, furtively held within the airtight code of silence unique to all-girl slumber parties. The boys surprised us by making reservations at a fancy restaurant in Georgetown, even securing their parents' luxury cars for our transportation. So far, the prom was promising to live up to all its hyped expectations; and Matt had chosen *me* to be his date, even under less-than-ideal circumstances.

Okay, so the whole night was a huge bust from minute one. Matt had his sullen eyes on Nina the entire time we were at the restaurant, each course prolonging my misery. And, if I remember correctly, I think Matt and Nina were on their way to getting back together, a turn of events that had happened sometime after he had asked me to the prom. This was indeed as unfortunate as it sounds. He made strained efforts to talk to me over our exquisite meals, kindling a sense of rejection that would fan into a full house fire by the time we reached the dance floor—a place that threatened even further insecurity considering I hadn't danced a step in my life. (Not unlikely for most pastors' kids I knew of back then.)

By the time we arrived at the hotel where our prom was being held, I already wanted out of the night as bad as I wanted out of the suffocating dress. And pearl earrings. And high heels—another thing my feet knew nothing of back then. My girl friends could see how Matt's indifference toward me was deflating my heart and self-respect into a shriveled prune, and they were surprisingly supportive for such normally immature ages. But no girl could offer me what I could only receive from a boy that night: the gift of being chosen, whether romantically or not. I have only shadowy memories of standing around the outskirts of the dance floor that night, though I think good ole Matt and I "danced" once out of sheer obligation. And, again, the whole thing is rather faint, but I'm pretty sure he asked Nina to dance near the end of the night—the final blow to an excruciating evening.

The next afternoon I tried to salvage with my family some positive vestiges of my humiliating experience, rehashing the night in our window-lit family room with spring dashing through the panes. Everyone wanted to know the decadent morsels of the evening, and I think I felt some sort of self-imposed expectation to relay them as somewhat successful and enjoyable. Though I do remember being fairly honest about Matt (as in I'd never go to another prom with him if it were being held in the Eiffel Tower overlooking the Seine), I didn't have the matured wisdom and perceptions I now have to discern everything I was feeling. But if I could distill my emotions into one concise concept, they could be summed up by the heartbreak of not being chosen.

Thankfully, Matt's rejection or just plain disinterest was not the only defining moment in my life, though it inflicted a healthy dose of pain. I had many more experiences that left me feeling similarly unchosen, woven with just as many when I felt picked and treasured. As far as we experience the depth of ache when we're not chosen, we experience the pure elation of joy when we are. And I'm glad I've experienced that wonderful feeling of being specifically desired and esteemed by different people, men and women alike, who I immensely respect and value. These are gifts.

wwwwwwwww

God understands our innate need to be chosen, presumably because He made us this way. He knows we long for someone to see us, to uniquely value our personalities and giftings, the way we toss our hair, or the inflections of our voices. (Perhaps nothing speaks to this more than God's institution of marriage, through the beauty of one man choosing one woman from the entire planet, and vice versa. How God knows about our need to be chosen and so generously planned for it.) This must be why God speaks over and over again throughout the pages of Scripture of the ways He has specifically chosen us:

> For you are a people holy to the LORD your God. The LORD your God has chosen you out of all the peoples on the face of the earth to be his people, his treasured possession. (Deut. 7:6)

> You did not choose me, but I chose you and appointed you to go and bear fruit—fruit that will last. (John 15:16)

In him we were also chosen, having been predes-
tined according to the plan of him who works out
everything in conformity with the purpose of his
will. (Eph. 1:11)

But we ought always to thank God for you, brothers loved by the Lord, because from the beginning
God chose you to be saved through the sanctifying
work of the Spirit and through belief in the truth.
(2 Thess. 2:13)

[We] who have been chosen according to the
foreknowledge of God the Father, through the
sanctifying work of the Spirit, for obedience to
Jesus Christ and sprinkling by his blood: Grace and
peace be yours in abundance. (1 Peter 1:2)

But you are a chosen people, a royal priesthood, a
holy nation, a people belonging to God, that you
may declare the praises of him who called you out
of darkness into his wonderful light. (1 Peter 2:9)

If I'm honest, the idea of being chosen by God doesn't always
seem as meaningful or monumental to me as I'd like, for several
reasons: He's God, so isn't loving and choosing people part of His
job? (Like a mother thinking her children are the most talented and
stunning people in the world—she's *supposed* to feel this way.) And
even though He has chosen me, He has also chosen countless others

since Adam. I'm not sure if being just one fleck of sand on the beach of chosenness makes me feel all that special and valued. Plus, I'm so accustomed to the idea of being chosen by people, flesh-and-blood humans, that I can find it difficult to palpably relish God's choosing of me, partly because I can't visibly see Him, audibly hear Him, or physically touch Him.

Yet when I am able to even slightly grasp God's choosing of me, my sentiments gravitate much more closely to David's when He exclaimed,

> When I consider your heavens,
>> the work of your fingers,
>> the moon and the stars, which you have set in
>> place,
> what is man that you are mindful of him,
>> the son of man that you care for him?
>> (Ps. 8:3–4)

It is only when my view of God is distinctly human and small that I think, *Well, God is supposed to choose me, right?* But when I understand even a fraction of His magnificence and greatness, I have the utter opposite response—one of disbelief and gratitude that the God who governs every atom of the universe has acquainted Himself with my unique being, lovingly and individually picking me with His mighty hands, holding me with the tenderness and awe of a child cupping his first sand dollar.

And when I consider Psalm 139 and meditate on the Lord's intimate knowledge of me, I begin to understand that I have not been mindlessly chosen as one soul in an enormous pack, like a rancher purchasing a herd of cattle. Instead, God has chosen me as a beloved individual who has been searched and known. Whose sitting and rising, and coming and going does not escape the roaming, never-slumbering eyes of God. He is familiar with all my ways, the words on my tongue before I speak them. His loving hand has hemmed me in on every side. I cannot rise to heaven or flee to hell or skip across the ocean without His presence attending me. And when I was in my mother's womb, and God was spinning planets and drawing the tide in and out, while He was dressing the fields and feeding the sparrows, He was—somehow at the same time—knitting together my fair skin and hazel eyes with my sensitive heart and melancholy temperament, stitching together threads of genes that science has yet to even identify. And while He sits on His throne, ruling and working, He thinks about me with vast and innumerable thoughts.

I think this is what it means to be chosen. And though we are part of a vast number of saints who have also been chosen, it does not in any way diminish the exclusivity of God's individual choosing of me—or you.

We can find Psalm 139 difficult to grasp because we may feel too sullied or flawed or sinful to ever be known and chosen by God in this way. How could He take this kind of specific interest in us when He knows our pasts and even our futures? How can He choose us when we house this inherent darkness we sometimes feel is part of the very fabric of our souls, something we can no more get rid of than our bones or ribs? But this is where we have to take the Bible for what it says, which is that Jesus came to seek and to save the sick and the lost, not the "healthy" and the "found." It's where we have to remember that Psalm 139 was written by King David, who stole a man's wife and then had the man killed. We are chosen not because we are perfect or always commendable but because of God's inexhaustible love for the world, and somehow, for just you and for just me. For "who will bring any charge against those whom God has chosen" (Rom. 8:33)?

So perhaps you are wondering if you have been chosen. Please do not be overcome with any fear that you are somehow disqualified or marked unchosen, because this would be to miss the good news of the gospel. I love what my Pastor Jim Thomas often preaches from his rickety music stand: "If you're worried that you're not chosen, become chosen today!" He is in no way trivializing the ancient and weighty doctrines of free will or election, yet his invitation is biblically grounded, for Christ will never turn away anyone who earnestly seeks Him. This is the simplicity of the gospel. Anyone who comes to Jesus to ask for forgiveness of sins, a right relationship with God, and eternity here (starting now) and in heaven receives this new life. And becomes gloriously chosen.

If you deeply struggle or remain unimpressed with God's choosing you, I encourage you to sit with a passage of Scripture like Psalm 139 and quietly receive its words. You may discover some lies you have told yourself, or someone else has told you, about never being worthy of God's choosing. You may have abuse or scars or sins that continually haunt the notion that you could ever be chosen. Whatever it may be, ask the Holy Spirit to show you what is standing in the way of your embracing such a comforting and freeing truth. It is the most liberating knowledge available to the human heart.

To attempt to live the virtues of compassion, kindness, humility, gentleness, patience, forgiveness, and joy is a ridiculous, maddening endeavor apart from this incredible gift of being chosen by God—as silly as thinking you're in the navy just because you've tried on the uniform. It takes the understanding and belief that God has seen us, known us, and lovingly chosen us to live the freeing life characterized by these traits. Suddenly, the virtues are no longer towering mountains we must figure out how to scale, but a journey God has chosen us for.

The power to take this journey is fueled by the holiness of God, the second truth Paul points out after his opening "Therefore." So now that we have a better handle on the truth that we have been chosen, we move on to a potentially more staggering proclamation: that we have been made holy. And if you happen to feel even less holy than chosen, it's okay—you can put on the uniform one sleeve at a time.

Pointy Sticks and Behavior Management

Holy

Last night I met a friend for tea at Casablanca in the Gulch, an artsy little neighborhood in downtown Nashville. Loose-leaf peppermint tea, to be certain, with half a banana nut muffin because I am trying to cut back on my white flour and refined sugar intake, though I've noticed the two are the best of friends and show up together in almost all my favorite foods. They look at me like, *We dare you to separate us.* One day I will find the courage to cut them off entirely.

From the outside, everything looked normal: a friend, a local coffee shop, my hot tea peering down on my devil muffin. It was the most standard of scenes. Yet little felt routine about this meeting as I struggled in my own skin and, strangely, in the most familiar of environments. I shifted a lot. Shelly is twenty-four, the mother of three, her oldest being eight. Her dad died when she was fifteen, and her mom is off smoking dope somewhere undisclosed. She sees her every so often, but encounters are intermittent at best. Drug users are like that—sea turtles who occasionally surface, only to plunge back into obscurity until the next sighting. Whether they mean to or not, they strand their loved ones on a shore of helplessness, leaving them to wonder where they'll pop up next: to the left, the right, how far away, or even at all? It's the most vicious and disheartening of scenarios.

Given my friend's upbringing, she too has been on drugs and has had her share of spins through the revolving door that gives entrance to jail or the outside world, depending on which way you're headed. I first met her at a Bible study I teach at her recovery program on Wednesday nights, a place where she's committed to living until she can figure a way out of the harrowing maze of addiction. I happen to believe that way out is Jesus, which is why I love being there on Wednesday nights as opposed to where I might otherwise be—on my couch, in front of the television, eating something that contains those two irritating best friends.

When I first asked Shelly why she started using, her answer seemed almost canned, as if she were preparing to play the "lost" character in a Sunday school skit: "To fill the profound emptiness and void I feel in my life." I was looking for the man behind the curtain holding up the St. Augustine script. I was genuinely stunned by the response of a twenty-four-year-old who'd had absolutely no exposure to the church, the Bible, or God. I've always heard people who'd met Christ later in life speak of a measure of emptiness in their previous years. I'm just not sure I'd ever heard someone actually articulate that emptiness in the middle of their pre-Christ vacuum.

This extreme void that Shelly expressed is what prompted our meeting. It was also the reason for my considerable unease.

Unease, not because of the drug abuse or jail time or colorful language or the smoke that is still lingering in my car. It was the curious tension that pulled between my being a committed Christian and my wrestling with how to talk about the simplicity of the gospel to someone who wanted to know but understood nothing of the language or constructs of the Christian faith. Even beyond her lack of framework, she pressed me with questions such as, "When you say God is the only one who can fill this emptiness, *how* does He fill it?" Or, "When you say God speaks, *how* do you hear Him? I want to read what's in the Bible, but *how* will I ever understand all these words and these stories?" As she sat across from me, throwing out every legitimate "how," I was charged by her pursuit but baffled in my response. After all these years of being in relationship with Jesus, I wanted to be able to explain things more clearly. The usual catchphrases that fly in a nodding group of like-minded individuals weren't working, and I couldn't dismiss my own discomfort.

I was certain that for any other Christian, Shelly's incredibly sincere questions would have been like a slow-pitched, oversized softball making its way to the giant good-news bat that even the daftest of believers couldn't help but nail out of the park. Why was I finding this to be such a struggle?

As I read several verses out of the books of Romans and 1 John, I found myself swimming in a sea of words like *justification, atonement, blood, cross, sanctification, sacrifice, righteousness.* Words that feel perfectly normal in Christian environments, like *pass the salt* or *Parmesan* feels at a dinner table, had suddenly become profoundly awkward and cumbersome. This very well could have been because these were entirely new concepts for Shelly, but I can't deny that some of the awkwardness stemmed from my lack of being able to tie these weighty words in to readily accessible truths. After dropping her off, I went home and processed my squirming and stammering. Could some of my unease have been my own lack of belief? Not general belief in the Christian faith, but faith that God has made me righteous in His sight, especially in those personal places of darkness—the ones that might not be so readily visible to the outside world but are glaringly obvious to my own soul? Surely you know what I'm talking about. Perhaps the cracks in my faltering confidence were from an anemic belief in justification, a pale understanding of how Christ has made me holy.

ⱮⱮⱮⱮⱮⱮ

While I was growing up, the Christian school I attended gave me a rudimentary understanding of how I had been justified through Jesus Christ, though this has not always been an easy concept for me to grasp deep down. I got into trouble for a lot of trivial things in an environment where the emphasis was more on behavior management than inward transformation.

To the front right of the classroom hung a string of cutout bubble letters that read:

> For by grace are ye saved through faith; and that not
> of yourselves: it is the gift of God: Not of works,
> lest any man should boast. (Eph. 2:8–9 KJV)

My Bible teacher referenced this verse with a slender pointy stick, telling us about Martin Luther and the Reformation and how this idea of God saving us apart from anything we could bring to the table was a truth that men and women had given their lives for in centuries past. It is the doctrine that separates Christianity from so many other religions, because it makes salvation about God loving us unconditionally, as opposed to about us trying to do more of some things and less of others, hoping we can gain His approval. Hoping we will one day be holy … enough.

The theology of being made righteous (justified) through Christ really is the most glorious of doctrines, and I'm grateful to the teachers who taught me this foundational truth. It's just that some of it got lost in the landscape of legalism where I spent much of my childhood. There was grace for eternal salvation with not a whole lot leftover for life on earth, which is where I could have really used it. You would not believe the variety of things for which I racked up thirty-three carbon-copied demerits while my parents were visiting missionaries in Europe. It was a rip-roaring time of gum-chewing and note-passing rebellion until my parents came home to the ominous pile of yellow slips on the banister. My pop was watching us kids and, passive man that he was, just let those things stack up like pancakes with nary a word, buying me Slurpees every day on the way home from school. But then my parents came home and real life commenced, where demerits were dealt with and Slurpees were no longer part of the equation. The reentry was rough, as my parents thumbed through all my transgressions over the past two weeks, racking their collective brains about what they were going to do with this feisty, strong-willed child who understood what it meant to be made holy for heaven but not as much for everyday life on earth.

Though I didn't readily grasp the far-reaching love of God in my junior high homeroom, it was within those walls and in association with Ephesians 2:8–9 where I first learned about the word *justification*—how through Jesus Christ, God had made me righteous in His sight. I am thankful that God allowed those tiny seeds about a lofty, five-syllable word (*justification*) to grow in the richer soil of life outside those classroom walls, life that would need pardoning for wrongs just a little more potent than sassiness, because of course there were heftier sins that followed my middle-school years, ones that I am thankful there are no carbon copies of floating around.

To quote scholar Wayne Grudem, "Justification is an instantaneous legal act of God in which he (1) thinks of our sins as forgiven and Christ's righteousness as belonging to us, and (2) declares us to be righteous in his sight."[1] When looking at the Christlike qualities we are to imbue in our lives, I think it's vital to begin with the concept of justification. How else would we ever display the virtues of Jesus if we have not first been clothed in His righteousness? Without this imputed righteousness (God thinking of Christ's righteousness as belonging to us), we are back to the concept of trying to clothe ourselves with clothes we don't actually own. Righteousness isn't something you can borrow either, just for the thrifty dressers out there.

〰〰〰〰〰〰

Countless volumes and commentaries have been written on the important doctrine of justification as it relates to the Christian faith, but my hope is that we may grasp it in its most distilled form. Otherwise we may find ourselves knowing much about it but not believing it for real life, something I have struggled with as recently as last week. It's sometimes hard to know what triggers past memories and regrets, but seemingly out of the blue I had begun to feel weighed down by old emotions. Almost overnight, I had gone from feeling like a zippy little dinghy to a tugboat dragging an old barge. I had this feeling of wanting a big do-over.

It was around this time I had a discussion with my editor, who said, "I find it so much easier to exude the characteristics of godliness when I am liberated by the truth of being made righteous in Christ." This is true. I couldn't have agreed with her more but confessed that this belief often challenges me the most. It's not always easy to believe that God sees me as perfectly righteous in Christ, especially since I know my own downfalls, my past, and myself. I happen to have been around for my whole life, so I know the underbelly of me. We each carry an array of experiences that defiles—or makes us feel defiled—in some manner, and it is precisely at these points that our belief in justification is challenged. Our past sins and choices, even abuses perpetrated upon us, are good at puncturing our belief that God has made us holy in His sight.

At the expense of losing all levity, consider that one thing you are most ashamed of. What memories does your brain spew out like a two-year-old spitting out sweet potatoes? Think of that moment or year or decade you so desperately wish you could have back. Sure, when the tip of the pointy stick strikes the cutout letters of Ephesians 2:8–9, the King James Version no less, you can quote it by heart and you can believe it for something as seemingly far off as heaven, but do you believe it for right now? For that moment you just thought back to or that season of far-off wandering? And if your answer is "No" or "I'd like to" or "I believe it for some things but not for others," you will have a hard time even thinking about humility, compassion, or any other virtue, because this fundamental truth must be settled before you make any attempts toward Christlikeness. Because believing that Jesus is our righteousness is the very fabric of every virtue. To be declared righteous and no longer guilty is the starting point, not just for a relationship with Jesus Christ but also for the power to live like Him.

I fear that we have inadvertently gotten all this jumbled: trying to muster up the willpower to eke out these virtues so we can be more righteous and holy, not the other way around. But this makes it about us and our ability to achieve the perfect righteousness that God demands, which is the opposite of justification by faith. In the gospel of Luke, Jesus eloquently speaks to this in the form of a story:

> To some who were confident of their own righteousness and looked down on everybody else, Jesus told this parable: "Two men went up to the temple to pray, one a Pharisee and the other a tax collector. The Pharisee stood up and prayed about himself: 'God, I thank you that I am not like other men— robbers, evildoers, adulterers—or even like this tax collector. I fast twice a week and give a tenth of all I get.' But the tax collector stood at a distance. He would not even look up to heaven, but beat his

breast and said, 'God, have mercy on me, a sinner.'
I tell you that this man, rather than the other, went
home justified before God." (Luke 18:9–14)

The two characters whom Jesus sketched were not random
selections but purposeful choices of two very distinct individuals:
the Pharisee, a picture of moral superiority, and the tax collector,
the emblem of shadiness and thievery. So how is it that the Pharisee
who displayed the disciplines of prayer, self-control (fasting), and
generosity (tithing) missed justification, while the shifty tax collector
who couldn't even crane his neck heavenward without divine mercy
went home justified? Because the Pharisee believed he could achieve
righteousness through his own goodness, and the tax collector realized it to be a gift solely from God.

Though this parable appears to be about salvation, it is essential
to the study of Christian virtues. Godliness does not begin with our
righteousness but with Jesus'. Because this act of imputed righteousness begins with Him, there's nothing we can do to mess it up. The
one thing we can do to circumvent it, however, is not to believe it.

I'm not talking about the kind of unbelief that is born out of
rejection of the gospel. For instance, I have the most energetic and
artistic friend who thinks that Christianity makes the most ridiculous assertion when it claims to be the only way to eternal life. She
does not believe that Jesus died for her sins, nor does she believe in
His forgiveness. She does not want Him to change her life. But this
is not the kind of unbelief I'm talking about. Rather I mean the "I
believe, help my unbelief!" kind, as found in Mark 9:24. I think
many of us live in this place of believing the verses about justification

that hang on the classroom walls of our minds, but we have trouble believing them in our actual lives.

Paul writes in Romans 6:11, "Reckon yourselves to be dead indeed to sin, but alive to God in Christ Jesus our Lord" (NKJV). The word *reckon* here implies counting or considering ourselves in this light—dead to sin but alive to God. When I least feel forgiven, I must reckon it so. I must take the resistant bull by its doubting horns and agree with God about the way He promises He sees me—clothed in the righteousness of Jesus. Chosen, holy, and loved.

∿∿∿∿∿∿∿

This past winter it snowed here in Nashville, a rarity considering I actually mean real snow. Upon first moving to town from Washington, DC, where I was fairly accustomed to snow (the kind that accumulates, anyway), I allowed my snow hopes to sail at the Nashville weathermen's predictions. I find that they are surprisingly accomplished at hooking you with any combination of the words *warning, roads, squalls, conditions, freezing, treacherous.* (*Treacherous* is a choice favorite. They know there's no way they're going to inspire an entire city to raid the grocery stores for bread and tomato soup if they don't use that word.) They lure us with animated penguins that dance across the screen in their cute little scarves, tugging on my sentimental love for crackling fires and the cozy cups of homemade hot chocolate that my dad used to brew over the stove while a billion white flakes flew outside our window. But I confess I have become jaded here in Tennessee. I have gone to bed after far too many of these big-storm-coming-soon declarations only to draw back the curtains the next morning to a view full of naked grass and pavement with the tiniest hint of frost on my car windshield.

So imagine my exceeding joy when last winter the entire town shut down because of a solid four inches of snow. (I might even go out on a limb and suggest we got five, depending on how your yard slopes.) And I do mean shut and bolted down, like only the pasta man from Philly's shop was open. So, of course, I went to see Tom and bought a box of spicy red-pepper linguine, fancied the cannoli, sniffed the cheeses, and commiserated with him about the south and their trifling "snow"—though I secretly love it here.

The first of the flakes had started the evening before, so I got to lie in bed and stare out the window at its light and effortless fall. I lost myself in its relentlessness, almost as if I were dodging meteoroids while flying through outer space. And once it started piling up on the ridge of my porch and the neighbors' roofs and the boughs of the trees, I became deeply thankful for justification. "'Come now, let us reason together,' says the LORD. 'Though your sins are like scarlet, they shall be as white as snow'" (Isa. 1:18).

Justification is a powerful truth closely intertwined with being made holy. It's why I wanted to back up with a cursory explanation of what it means to be justified, because justification undergirds the meaning of the holiness Paul speaks of in Colossians. A holiness that means to be set apart. It means that God has cupped His hand around me and slid me over from the natural, selfishly propelled world. He has set me apart for Himself and for the purposes He longs to accomplish in and through my life, partly to labor with Him in redeeming this natural, selfishly propelled world.

The Greek word for *holy* in Colossians 3:12 is related to the word for *saint*. It is a beautifully endearing description of how God has taken us as very desperate sinners and formed us into saints. To be set apart for God as one of His saints is a really different concept from seeing the word *holy* and suddenly thinking we need to flutter our wings and don our halos, flinging righteousness around like fairy dust fashioned by our own hands. The fact that God has set us apart will absolutely include profound change, but our efforts in this change come after our justification. Again, I think this is why Paul says we are chosen, holy, and loved *first*, reminding us that *since* we are chosen and set apart as special and unique individuals, we are then to live like it by putting on the virtues. These virtues that Paul invites us to wear will help us look like what we already are.

∿∿∿∿∿∿∿

I think we as the church, generally speaking, have gotten this idea of being set apart a bit confused with being set against. Now, you have to know I love the church. I am not writing as a skeptic, because the church at its finest is an institution of reconciliation for the lost and broken, and I have nothing if I have not the church. However, I think we would do much better as a whole if we focused more on compassion, kindness, humility, gentleness, and patience than on how all the non-Christians are ruining society with their bad behavior and politics. D. L. Moody said, "A holy life will produce the deepest impression. Lighthouses blow no horns; they only shine."[2] I'm afraid that at this moment in Western history, at least as far as the watching world is concerned, often the church is clanging like a deafening cymbal and holding forth a light that is but a flickering flame.

It's much easier to blow our moral police horns on all those transgressors running around than it is to live penetrating lives of holiness. We can criticize without even stretching, but let us try running the marathon of patience. We can gossip without expending a whit of energy, but what would it look like to speak words of kindness to those who accuse and tear us down? Being set apart by living the virtues of Colossians 3:12 is hard! This may be why some of us carry our bullhorns in our backpacks and purses—ungodly judgmentalism is the far easier thing to do. But how many of us are actually glowing, guiding the lost amidst the storm and fog, drawing them near to Jesus with the light of the gospel rather than blasting them with our condemning foghorns?

This is not to say we emasculate words like *love* and *compassion* and *kindness* to limp, amoral platitudes that don't stand for truth or righteousness and don't point in any definitive direction. I love what Dallas Willard preaches: that loving others is about giving them that which is for their good, not necessarily what they desire. The virtues are not deceptive enablers that encourage those around us to live any way they wish; instead, they are a strong light that blazes in the midst of ever-increasing darkness, calling the lost and cold—even in the Christian community—to warm themselves by its fire. The church clothed in the virtues is a church whose light is always on, distinct from the darkness (certainly opposed to unrighteousness), but perhaps known more for what it is for rather than all it is against.

This is true not just on a corporate church level but also in our personal lives. We are called to live in a way that is set apart, that is worthy of a saint. And of course holiness doesn't mean being set apart to be ineffective or sidelined, like pulling a figurine out of a box and placing it on a shelf to motionlessly sit there. There's an active meaning to our set apartness. We are to be sacred, pure, and upright so we can shine brightly as the light of the world, as a city on a hill that cannot be hidden (Matt. 5:14). But again, we have to be clear that trying to live out the brightness of the virtues doesn't make us holy; rather, because we have already been made holy (set apart), we get to put on the clothes of virtue.

I love this idea because I long to live differently. Not piously or legalistically, 'cause that's just the kind of thing that will put me in counseling faster than you can spend $110 an hour. But in a world where we are governed by selfish ambition and impatience and "don't tell me what to do" and anger that flares up like an infection, how I yearn to live altogether differently, not simply because I've learned how to manage my behavior but because God has changed me from the inside. And because I desperately desire to draw others to Jesus by a life that is distinctly bright and whole, because He has made it so.

Paul writes, "But now he has reconciled you by Christ's physical body through death to present you *holy* in his sight, without blemish and free from accusation" (Col. 1:22). Paul clearly says that our being chosen, set apart as a saint, and loved is the sole work of God. We will get to our part of the process soon enough—the part where we start dressing in forgiveness, peace, kindness, humility, compassion, patience, and joy. But for now, we must accept and enjoy the grace and the justification that has set us apart. We must revel in being saints. Anything less, and we're back to demerits and striving and classroom lectures, things that may manage our behaviors but can never change our hearts. And if being chosen, holy, and loved is about anything, it is about our hearts.

Father Loves You

Loved

I am in my thirties and thankful to write that I now have a front porch. A real adult one. It overlooks a patchy yard (mine), a few houses from the 1930s drizzled with succulent landscaping, and an African American church that boasts the most colorful suits and dazzling hats you've ever seen go in and out of a place.

The furniture on my porch is ridiculous, though: I have one swinging chair that is missing a plastic strap underneath its faded cushions, so if I forget to warn my unsuspecting guests to sit with caution, they may momentarily lose their breath if they settle in too confidently. I've got a vintage red chair that has a hole in the fake leather so when you sit down there's a chance the spring will claw its way through the tear, cleverly grabbing the back of your pants—something you let happen to you only once. My friends are protesting another summer of having to deal with what has now been affectionately coined the "butt-grabber." I'm saving my quarters as if for a trip to Europe—have you seen how much outdoor furniture costs these days?

But I love my porch, even with all its flaws. It's a place I can steal away to, especially when I want to be enveloped by the warm breeze, serenaded by the chirping birds. Sometimes I just sit alone and stare silently, languorous and happy for the respite from anything and everything electronic. Occasionally, my neighbor Frances moseys over for a relaxed chat peppered with benign neighborhood gossip—she's always got the scuttlebutt (not to be confused with what happens if you sit in the red chair). And if I can concentrate with all the buzzing of mowers and mosquitoes, I love to read out there. It's a rejuvenating rectangle of tranquility that I never knew I would delight in so deeply.

Last year sometime, well before this book was in the works, I nestled myself on the porch with my Bible, sifting for consolation after feeling particularly unchosen by a friend. It wasn't someone terribly close to me but with enough relational proximity to lodge a sting. I was working my way through Colossians and happened to come across the "dearly loved" piece of Paul's writing in 3:12. Now, I can't tell you why certain words or phrases in Scripture excitably spring out at me in some instances, while at other times they seem to lie there dusty and flat, but this was one of those reach-out-and-grab-me moments. I felt as if God Himself were speaking to me on my front porch—but certainly not sitting on any of the furniture—telling me directly that He didn't just love me but *dearly* loved me.

It was one of those breaths when I really got it, when I felt palpably chosen and especially dear to my Father. I knew He saw me and the rejections I had sustained, even if they were minor compared to the much deeper sufferings of others. I knew that He cared for how I was hurting and that all His affection for me sprang out of His vast and lavish love for *me*.

Just the reminder that I am beloved of God gave me the nurture and confidence to put the trifling wound in its proper place and get on with my day. *I am loved and chosen by God;* what else did I need to know? The problem is we either hear we are loved by God so much that it starts to lose its meaning, or we've watered down our understanding of *agape* (one of the biblical words for *love*) to the point that it starts ringing ordinary. Familiarity may breed contempt, but a lot of times it just breeds numbness.

vvvvvvvvvvv

I have a dear Brazilian friend who runs a ministry along the Amazon. She speaks English well, though she makes a syllable out of the *-ed* of every word that ends with those two letters. For example, when she says something freaked her out, she says it freak-*ed* her out. And if she uses the word *helped*, she pronounces it help-*ed*. Selfishly, I hope she will never advance beyond those pronunciations, because there's one word she speaks that I don't want my ears to grow too accustomed to: when she looks me at me and my friends with her wild Brazilian eyes and says, "I have love-*ed* you so much!" Because, let's face it, being love-*ed* is so much richer than being just plain old loved.

Just the way she says it makes me think about the word *loved* with novelty. Paul does a little of this same thing when he writes that we are "dearly loved" or "beloved," depending on your translation. The Greek verb is *agapao* (related to the noun *agape*), and it means "to have a preference for, wish well, regard the welfare of … the love which led Christ, in procuring human salvation, to undergo sufferings and death." When talking about an object, the word means "to welcome with desire, long for."[1] When we understand this definition of love, we know that we are affectionately cared for, that our well-being is important to God, so much so that He gave us His Son on this earth to die on a cross, then resurrected Him so we could be in relationship with Him.

The fact that we use the same English word *love* to describe how we feel about chocolate or diamonds or new porch furniture seems pale and silly; it renders the English language weak in such instances. So it is helpful when we can pause and let love's meaning wash over us anew. Perhaps this is why Paul emphasized that we are *dearly* loved, while prefacing it with being chosen and made holy, because these additional truths set God's incredible love for us well apart from any other love we may speak of or know.

Our belief and understanding of God's love for us is essential to having a life that vibrantly expresses the virtues. If we don't really believe we are dearly loved—or love-*ed*, Brazilian style—we will have an impossible time fitting into the clothes of compassion, kindness, humility, gentleness, patience, forgiveness, peace, and joy. For it is out of the unfathomable riches of Christ's love for us that all these characteristics become attainable virtues: First, because His love gives us a new life, literally allowing us to cast off our selfish natures and clothe ourselves in the character of Christ. Second, because knowing we're loved gives us the confidence and freedom to live in this new way. When we know and believe God loves us, the biblical virtues are no longer like school uniforms we begrudgingly put on but exquisite clothing we are eager to slip into. When we are confident we are loved, Paul's list of Christlike characteristics becomes less chores and more delights we are eager to embody, because we trust the ways in which God has called us to live. We understand that these characteristics will not only bless those around us but will be beneficial for us as well. This is all a distant cry from moralism or behavior management.

∿∿∿∿∿∿∿

This morning I was listening to a message by a brilliant theologian and gentle pastor (both the same guy, which is a real delight to get in one human). He spoke about Colossians 3 in connection with taking off the old self and putting on the new. (More on this to come.) He explained that a great burden is released from us when we come to understand that it is *safe* to live the way God intends for us to live. At first, telling the truth doesn't always feel safer than lying; blessing our enemies doesn't always seem like a better idea than cursing them. But when we begin to believe that God's ways of virtuous living are better than our own, we start to grasp that it is truly better to love than to hate, to be merciful than to condemn, to be patient than to be angry. We begin to trust Him.

Love and trust are inextricably linked. We will hardly be motivated to live the way Christ desires for us to live if we don't trust

Him. And how can we trust Him if we don't believe He loves us? I'm not talking about the vague, head-knowledge type of love—the kind that believes Jesus died for our sins and loves us in some religious, universal sense—but the belief in an intimate love that is passionate and personal. Never have I come up against a greater obstacle in my own heart than this pervasive "inability" to believe Jesus truly and deeply loves me. Though I grew up in a loving and close-knit family, I understood God's love as something that hinged more on my performance than on an anchor of unconditional affection and commitment. I perceived that His love had more to do with how well I could manage my sin or behavior than with His immutable pursuit of me.

There are many other reasons why we have difficulty grasping God's love for us. It could be the broken homes so many have grown up in, never experiencing the rapturous hugs of a father or the nurturing touches of a mother. It may stem from volcanic wounds like a harrowing rape or betrayal or bitter divorce that has left us hollow and seemingly unable ever to believe in something as fairy-tale as real love.

Last night I sat in a restaurant with a woman who told me that she hasn't heard the words "I love you" in over four years, the last time being when her son called her shortly before he was killed in an accident. I felt detached from such an astonishing revelation, unable to imagine a life without parents or friends telling me on a regular basis how much they love me. Sure, it would be nice to hear this from a husband eventually, but not hearing it *at all* is altogether unfathomable. It made me expectant for what will happen in the coming weeks as this new friend begins to understand that God dearly loves her—and that her new community in the church loves her as well. I am eager to watch *agape* astound her long-forsaken heart.

I once caught an interview of a man who cheated on his wife multiple times. When asked why he threw away such an amazing marriage and family, he said it was because he never thought anyone was capable of truly loving him. His way of dealing with the false belief that he could never be loved was to sabotage everything he had through torrid affairs. We may or may not identify on such a level, but most of us can relate to feeling like we've messed up way too badly for anyone, especially God, to really love us. Maybe tolerate or brusquely excuse us, but not zealously love us.

And none of this is to mention the pressures that the press and Hollywood sling on our backs, constantly telling us that if we really want to be loved, we'd better figure out how to make piles of money or trim our waists down to an impossible size, plump up some of our other features, manipulate a powerful career—or at the very least, seize all the material goods we can get our hands on so someone will finally notice us, need us, become attached to us, maybe even *love* us. We have turned love into something we can earn as opposed to something that is freely given, unflagging, based on covenant, and not hinging merely on whims and return investments.

Many of us do not know how to rest in the *agape* love of Jesus. We're always waiting for the other shoe to drop or for the loan to come due—we're pretty sure there's a catch to love. We've been conditioned to be suspect of God, plagued by an unhealthy fear of Him (not the biblical kind of fear), wondering when the boom is going to be lowered. We're not used to the kind of authentic and unconditional love that the Bible speaks of. We either don't believe God loves us this way, or we put Him in His own category, allowing for a type of unconditional "God-love" but somewhat invalidating it as distant and religious, a love that doesn't count in our real lives.

But what happens to us when we really get it? When the flower of our hearts begins to unfold under a covenant love? When we're not waiting to be leveled but can trust the heart of God? When we can lean into the virtues as freeing and distinguished ways to live life as opposed to confining, legalistic actions that are meant to garner God's approval? This is a shift God has been directing in my life over the past many years. I don't understand all the reasons why His love has been so difficult for me to grasp, but I will tell you that as I have been able to see it and believe it, I've never experienced anything else as powerful or liberating.

The adjustment in my understanding has not come overnight. I have been on a steady pursuit of God's love for many years, looking for its manifestation in the lives of dynamic believers, highlighting remarkable expressions of it in Scripture, and praying for it often. And, of course, as soon as I write that I have been on a steady pursuit of God's love, I am keenly aware that His love has been on a steady pursuit of me—before I was even formed in my mother's womb. Still, I can put no number on the amount of times I have asked Him to show me His love in very deep and intimate ways that let me know His personal affection for me. I have prayed that He would help me stop trying to wrangle His love by my effort, that I could take a deep breath and fall back on the immovable truth that His love for me is without condition. And when the sufferings and tragedies of this world seem to yell in the face of such love, I hope for His transcendent presence that doesn't always explain but never forsakes.

⋀⋁⋀⋁⋀⋁⋀⋁

I don't know if you know anyone who gets this love in the core of his or her soul, but seeing a person rest soundly in the love of God is a marvel to behold. You would think this would be readily obvious in most every Christian, but I have found such deep abiding rare. In particular, I knew one person who exemplified this quiet rest, a man who sadly died of a heart attack just a couple weeks after I saw him at my grandfather's funeral. None of us understood why God took J. R. so early. He was such a beacon of inspiration to everyone around him. He was especially an encouragement to my dad, who can get easily weighed down by the burdens a pastor is bound to bear. If there was anything J. R. was really against, it was the silly act of striving, something he always encouraged my dad and the rest of us to refrain from—precisely because, according to him, it's the most unnecessary of struggles when you have a loving heavenly Father.

J. R. always referred to God as Father—not *the* Father, just Father. As in, "Don't worry so much, Kelly, just ask Father about it." Somehow it never seemed weird or self-aggrandizing when he said it but came off as striking and sincere, like this guy really knew the Lord in a tender and authentic way. He had a habit of writing notes to people that spoke of God's love for them, tucking them in sock drawers and glove compartments, peppering reminders wherever he could. He was a certified counselor, but you could forget the square office and sixty-minute time limit. J. R. was known for meeting with people for hours, more comfortable counseling on a mountain's trail than from across a table—unless that table happened to be in a coffee shop. His message never changed. It was always something related to "Father loves you."

I wish J. R. were still here, because the confidence he had in God's love was infectious, as if you could almost grip it with your bare hands when you were around him. Of course, this love is not available only to people like J. R.; it's just that he had a special understanding of it that uniquely manifested itself. And this understanding always led to a natural outcropping of the virtues. He was extremely merciful, patient, kind, gentle, compassionate, giving, and most definitely joyful. And I know for certain this was because he deeply grasped the love of God, the true source of every Christlike characteristic there is.

The truth of God's love for me has been a revelation that has unfolded over time, something that continually seeks out new crevices in my ever-doubting heart. As I walk with the Lord through the sultry deserts and verdant peaks that are characteristic of this life, I am grasping His affection with grander measures.

If I can offer any prodding from my own life, perhaps even a note from J. R., it would be to pray that God would help you see His love and understand it more fully (Matt. 7:7–8). I believe God delights in answering these prayers. Also, I would look for sightings of His love in Scripture, and I would highlight the words that speak most powerfully to you. Then, the trick is to hold fast to those verses when you're feeling especially doubtful and dull, and let them be the final word over your fickle emotions and waning beliefs. And, certainly not least, look for others who are passionately in love with

Jesus, because they understand that He is passionately in love with them. We were designed for relationship with men and women and children who cling to Christ, who will douse us with cold water on a hot day, telling us and showing us that God loves us even in the places where we have ceased believing it. These interwoven threads of prayer, Scripture meditation, and fellowship will bind our experiences of God's intimate love for us. In the meantime, the thought of living the virtues will strangely grow from duty to delight.

Chosen, holy, loved. The measurements are in and the character clothes are going to fit. The wardrobe is ours. There is only one more step, as it were, to donning the virtues that hang liberally within our reach. Our old vices and habits must go. The petty practices we've worn, the bland shades of bitterness with our beads of resentment, all of it must go. Shoved into bags and left on the curbside so we're not tempted to try them on again in four years when we can't find a *thing* to wear! We must ready ourselves for the fitting room where the curtain is drawn and the old is doffed. Where we slip into something altogether new. And when we emerge, only God knows what we will look like—I suppose *beautiful* will have something to do with it.

5

The Angel in the Stone

Taking Off the Old

I was only thirteen years old and, I'm afraid, much more taken with the mounds of rigatoni and endless vats of olive oil than I was with the towering sculpture of a man whose sculptor, incidentally, forgot to chisel him clothes. It was a real mystery to me: looping lines of all nationalities clamoring to see this world-renowned statue of a guy named David, who was completely naked best I could tell. Further mystifying was that the whole lot of us could have been outside in the Tuscan sun licking our gelato or diving five layers deep into a slice of tiramisu. I wasn't sure what the comparison was really. And so I framed up the situation once more, weighing the two options on the imaginary but historically accurate scale in my head: Carbs, naked guy? Carbs, naked guy? It ended up being a record-shattering win for carbs—exactly what I had predicted. Yet by the intent looks of the people still standing in line to see this David, I could only infer that everyone had already had their gnocchi, gelato, or cream puffs for the morning. My thirteen-year-old mind could think of no other explanation.

I have yet to return to Italy, though I have tentative plans to travel there in the near future—this time, a touch older. Ironically enough, if I do get the opportunity to stroll upon the cobblestone streets of Florence again, I will no doubt find my way back into that long and twisty line leading to the feet of Michelangelo's *David*. After all, a lot has changed since I was thirteen. I am wiser and more learned and have a much deeper appreciation for art and culture and anything that has endured the unrelenting hand of time. Don't be ridiculous; I will have eaten my ladyfingers first, but I will be back to see him.

Not all was lost that day in the Accademia Gallery, as I stood there with my mom, who had bravely and graciously decided to let her firstborn miss the first two weeks of high school so I could travel to Milan on a missions trip. I honestly never caught up those two weeks—I chased them all the way through my senior year—but that trip was what started me singing and playing the guitar for people outside of my family. (There's nothing like leading worship songs in Italian—or *I*-talian as my grandparents pronounce it—with a church band in the public squares of the duomos to get one poised for a career in music. We weren't afraid to exercise our use of the tambourine, either.)

I had the opportunity to see what Christianity looked like in an entirely different country, where it hadn't faded into the fabric of the culture like it can in the States, but garishly popped against the backdrop of thickly layered curtains of religiosity—or total agnosticism—that characterize so much of Europe. I encountered stories in Italy different from ones I had heard in Virginia, from people who had been completely transformed by the light of Jesus. Stuff you just don't get in algebra I, so thank you, Mom, for taking me with you. My first two weeks of freshman year can still wait.

And though Michelangelo's many works were slightly lost on me at the time, I have always hung on to the unique process of sculpting: While most artists create by adding *to* something, a sculptor creates by taking away. Michelangelo himself said, "I saw the angel in the marble and carved until I set him free." To Michelangelo, every conceivable creation lay within the confines of a block of marble; he only had to take away the excess—in all the exact right places, of course—until he uncovered the desired image he could already see perfectly complete in his mind.

This is much how I envision the idea of taking off the old self, which Paul speaks of in Colossians 2:11: "In [Christ] you were also circumcised, in the *putting off of the sinful nature,* not with a circumcision done by the hands of men but with the circumcision done by Christ." It may seem odd to pair throwing off our old selves with the process of circumcision. But these images come together when you consider that circumcision was a Jewish practice that signaled God's covenant with Israel as His chosen people. When Paul refers to circumcision here, he tangibly conveys a cutting away of the flesh (or self), something Christ did for us when He came and blew open the doors of the gospel to all nations. Now Jews and Gentiles alike have access to a new kind of circumcision: one that is not physical but spiritual.

Warren Wiersbe, in his commentary on Colossians, contrasts the physical circumcision of the Jews with the spiritual circumcision for all believers: Jewish circumcision was an external surgery that affected only part of the body. It was performed by human hands and lacked spiritual help for conquering sin. Spiritual circumcision is an internal process that affects the heart by cutting away the whole "body of sins." It is done without human hands and enables us to overcome sin. Wiersbe sums this up nicely when he says, "What the law could not do, Jesus Christ accomplished for us.... The old sinful nature is not eradicated, for we can still sin (1 John 1:5—2:6). But the power has been broken as we yield to Christ and walk in the power of the Spirit."[1]

All of this is important to our growing in the virtues, because it sets the foundation for the process of dying to our old selves. It's hard to show compassion if we haven't first taken off anger, pretty impossible to forgive if we're rotting in our bitterness, difficult to be humble if we're drenched in pride. In essence, the truth presented in Colossians 2:11 grants us the chisel to start chipping away at these soul enemies, the power to begin the sanctification process. Without the death and resurrection of Christ, we would have no power, tools, or resources to excise the parts of ourselves that manipulate and lust and steal and become jealous and gossip and overeat and fly off the handle. So when seeking to live the virtues, we first must be aware of the work that is solely *His*: "God made [us] alive with Christ" (Col. 2:13).

〰〰〰〰〰

But living a new life requires a mysterious team effort here—some tactile exertion on the part of the players, not just the coach. If you look ahead to Colossians 3:5–10, you see that Paul encourages *us* to put to death sexual immorality, impurity, lust, evil desires, and greed. He also tells *us* to rid ourselves of anger, rage, malice, slander, filthy language, and lying. Lastly, he states that *we* have "taken off [our old selves] with its practices." But, as mentioned before, none of this would be possible if we didn't have chapter 2 of Paul's letter, which deals with what God has done to free us from sin and the law. (It also wouldn't be possible without the power and ever-present help of the Holy Spirit, which is covered in Galatians 5.) So when it comes to virtuous living, both God and we are at work.

The merging of God's work and our work has always been a bit confusing to me. I can passably spit out the concept if pressed, but it becomes fuzzier when I'm actually attempting to live out this new life. I think this is because it's difficult to judge our own progress and weigh our own motives on our personal journeys of sanctification. Since our transformation happens over time, it can be difficult to harness concrete measurements of change. Not to mention, God fashions His character in us in different ways at different times. I have had experiences when He has simply gifted me with an extra measure of a certain virtue in a certain situation, and other instances when He has used refining circumstances and people to develop a virtue in my life over an excruciating amount of time. (I far prefer when He uses the former route.) Mingle the myriad ways that God builds our character along with our own choices to obey or disobey Him, and you've got a process that can be hard to detail. God's movements and our obedient responses run together in a way that contributes to a life that looks more like the image of Christ, but how we all get there—where we're at play, where God is at play—is less clear to me.

I've been to Brazil a couple of times, and one of the most fascinating splendors of nature that I've witnessed there is the Meeting of the Waters. This is where the Negro and the Solimões rivers come together to form the Amazon River. Because the two rivers originate from different places, flow at different speeds, have different temperatures, density, and colors, when they converge, they don't actually mix for over six miles. Though I am certain there are far more eloquent descriptions of this stunning stretch of the Amazon, the Negro looks like a body of Coca-Cola and the Solimões like a rush of milky coffee. Together they make up an oil-and-water-like separation that neither is willing to relinquish, at least for a few miles. They keep to themselves in a breathtaking display of what resembles two horizons running side by side, technically as one river, until finally they visibly blend into each other to form arguably the greatest river in the world.

The perplexing piece is that while they become one river—the Amazon—at the point where they meet, they don't look like it for a while. And though this is not a theologically foolproof analogy, I have to say that the longer I know Jesus, the more I witness the blend. When I first came into relationship with Christ, understanding my need for a Savior and believing in Him for salvation, my life joined with His. It was my personal "meeting of the waters" where I was justified and my life became hidden in Christ's. Even though I was very young, my life didn't look so much like His. We were like two rivers now headed in the same direction, but initially I had different desires, tendencies, habits, and practices. It took time before my life started to look like Christ's, before you could tell I was being conformed into His image. (And, of course, this is a lifelong process.)

Though my old life and its practices may have looked distinctly different from Christ's, as time passed, my heart and longings began to dissolve further and further into His. I can't specifically point out all the exact places and ways this has happened—where God moved, where I obeyed in response—any more than I can pinpoint where and how the Negro and the Solimões finally coalesce into a seamless blend of color, temperature, properties, and speed. I just know that eventually they do.

〰〰〰〰〰

Despite this mystery, I believe Scripture is clear that virtuous living requires effort on our part. As Dallas Willard so insightfully says, "Grace is not opposed to effort (action)—though it is opposed to earning."[2] When we take the chisel to the stone of our old natures, there's one piece in Colossians 3:9 that adds practical instruction for us: Paul says to take off the old self *with its practices*. We practice things all day long without always realizing it. The question becomes not *are* we practicing, but *what* are we practicing? It's easy to get stuck in the pattern of our old lifestyles when we don't change our practices. Without coming at this from a legalistic perspective, we must make some tangible changes when we're learning to walk in the Spirit.

I don't know what this looks like for you, but in my own life I have had to stop "practicing" gossip. When the urge arises to critique, assess, share—even if the words "bless her heart" are attached—I practice something else in its place, something more like restraint. I've had to let go of certain television shows, movies, music, and magazines that stir up or bolster my selfish appetite. I love to be entertained, but I can no longer justify the kinds of amusement that push or support my "old life." (And when I refer to my "old life," because I met Christ at a very early age, I'm not referring to my pre-Christ days but to habits and ways that don't delight Him.)

A new development that I've noticed is that I don't even want to justify these things anymore, as my desires have actually changed (again, part of the supernatural process I can't always put my finger on). There are certain places I don't go anymore, places that coddle small thinking and thin pleasures. In good conscience I can't practice anger by giving in to explosions or reckless words. I can't practice greed or pride or bitterness without feeling the rub of the Holy Spirit. This doesn't mean I am never angry, proud, or selfish. It just means these old ways of living aren't my everyday habits.

ᴧᴧᴧᴧᴧᴧᴧᴧᴧ

When we strive for holiness, it can be our propensity to whip out our carving tools and start tapping our hammers somewhat aimlessly, hoping we'll discover something truly magnificent even if accidentally. But before we start chiseling, we have to know what must be chipped away so we can eventually get to the angel in the stone. In the New Testament, we see a lot of specific things that God lovingly forbids listed; many of them appear in Colossians: sexual immorality, greed, lust, anger, rage, slander, lying, and so on. The Bible gives us clarity for what ungodly characteristics we should remove from our lives, convicting us of things that are not always so obvious. This is why Scripture meditation and study is so vital to our spiritual health. Prayer is also essential, creating space for the Holy Spirit to do His cleansing and convicting work in our hearts.

And, of course, we will always need family and friends who will speak truth into our lives, people who can shed a little light on what they perceive to be some of our more notable obstacles and struggles. I am grateful for close friends and family who can speak these occasionally hard words to me, because the wounds from a friend are much better than the kisses of an enemy (Prov. 27:6).

All of these assist us in putting aside old practices, and this putting aside is an essential starting point for a life characterized by the Christian virtues. It's hard to effectively practice the characteristics of godliness while we're still clinging to other practices that war against them. It's difficult to get to the virtues if you haven't first chiseled back certain things like insecurity or hurry or worry or greed or impatience, just as you can't have an exquisite sculpture without first knocking off all the pieces of stone that don't belong. You can't put on the "new woman" without taking off the old one.

Or, as Michelangelo put it, "Carving is easy, you just go down to the skin and stop." Living the biblical virtues is just as ridiculously simple: Chip off the aforementioned foes until you've hit the skin of godliness, and bingo, you're there. Okay, so this is easy only if you can wield a chisel like Michelangelo or harness holiness like a Puritan, but at least we know what we're after here.

Relinquishing the old, starving the flesh, ceasing from certain practices. It's not the breeziest of processes, but it is a clearing out, a slimming down that makes us ready for the fitting room—a place where we can slip into the virtues with greater ease and more tailored results. In essence, because we have been made alive in Christ, we have also been given the power to dress altogether differently. But we must exercise this power as a sculptor exercises his chisel, working to reach the core of the beauty and freedom of the character of Christ.

In the pages ahead we will look at some of the specifics of this character clothing as detailed in Colossians 3:12–17. We'll look at compassion, kindness, humility, patience, forgiveness, peace, and joy. This is not an exhaustive list of the virtues, nor will I treat the virtues I'm writing about exhaustively. An accomplished writer friend of mine recently told me never to write from a distance—some of the best writing advice I have ever received. So I will only write about the following virtues in a way I understand and have experienced—or at least hope to experience. I will steer clear of what I think I'm "supposed" to say about them and leave the loftier renderings on the virtues to the scholars and ancients. (Their works are amazing and essential, but if I tried to mimic them, you would inevitably sense the *distance*.) What I promise to give you is honesty, story, and my sincerest understanding of what Scripture has to say about clothing ourselves in the character of Christ. An offering I hope will keep us from merely flowing alongside His glorious life, but will make us altogether look like Him.

The Perfect Storm

Forgiveness, Part 1

Forgiveness. It is one of those virtues that, when we try to implement it, can paradoxically feel noble and hopeful and nearly like drinking poison. But when true forgiveness has its time to work into every wounded crevice of our being, we find that what once tasted like straight vanilla extract was actually a balm that cleansed the bitterness, leaving new and tender places from which life could grow free from the cords of anger and obsession. In other words, letting someone off our hook for all the terrible hurt he or she has inflicted is one of the more gut-wrenchingly painful things we will ever do, while the simultaneous release of casting off our bitterness and angst is one of the sweetest forms of freedom we will ever know.

The Bible tells us a lot about forgiveness, but it also shows us a lot in the form of stories, offering insight for those who will look closely. Since forgiveness is deeply personal and always involves relationship, these stories allow us to watch forgiveness being worked out in the lives of real people who experienced real wounds. This is helpful for those of us who have a pretty good handle on what forgiveness is but have a harder time actually implementing it. I know a little of skydiving, but I'd prefer never to strap a parachute on my back and thrust myself out of a plane so I can barrel toward earth at the speed of gravity multiplied by my weight until, one desperately hopes, the parachute opens. Knowing and doing are quite different.

When we revisit Colossians 3:12–14, we find Paul encouraging us to put on forgiveness after listing the following select virtues from our spiritual wardrobe: compassion, kindness, humility, gentleness, and patience. I think it's interesting that Paul found it sufficient to simply name these first five but paused for a moment to let the next virtue of forgiveness breathe: "Bear with each other and forgive whatever grievances you may have against one another. Forgive as the Lord forgave you." Paul didn't expound on any of the other virtues in this particular passage, but when it came to forgiveness, he must have figured a little more encouragement was needed, a small nod to the potential agony of this one. It's as if he knew we'd need the extra boost over the high fences of bitterness or grudge holding.

Tonight was my Wednesday-night Bible study at the recovery program I work with downtown. Right now I have a group of three angry women, along with one kind but slightly self-righteous woman who, tonight, was dressed in a pink sweat suit. After one of the angry women let a few swearwords fly, the friendlier lady asked her to please refrain from using such language during spiritual-emphasis class. For a brief moment I thought the pink lady was going to get lynched, even though her request was legitimate and probably should have come from me first. I am still learning how to lead this group.

These are courageous women who are working hard to overcome their addictions after being freed from incarceration. I've rotated through several different groups, and never have I come up against a tougher mob than this one. (And I use the term *mob* in the most affectionate of ways.) I now see why the Bible refers to the Word of God as a sword, because I actually felt like I was whipping it through the air tonight. In some ways it even felt more like an ice pick, chipping away at years and years of abuse, mind-altering substances, and raw anger. At moments I'd sense a couple of chips breaking loose here and there, but all things considered, I felt like I shut the door on an iceberg tonight. I'm pretty sure the agent that's keeping this iceberg rock solid is the freezing temperature of unforgiveness.

And I don't just mean the women's unwillingness to forgive others, but more important, their unwillingness to accept the forgiveness of Jesus for themselves. Because the first can't truly happen before the second. (Forgive as Christ forgave you.) I used to read Paul's admonishment to forgive others as Christ has forgiven us as a way of almost having to keep up with the Lord. Be as good as Him. Sort of like your mom saying, "Look, your dad ate his peas; you need to eat yours too." But I think that's to miss the point entirely. When we experience the kindness of God that leads us to repentance, when we understand that no good thing dwells within us, when the staggering weight of our guilt is lifted because of what Jesus Christ has done and we sense the shame of our pasts fleeing as far as the east is from the west, our hearts soften. They stretch. We find we have compassion for others (bear with each other and forgive whatever grievances you have with one another), in ways we never dreamed possible.

The command to forgive others as Christ forgave us is not a lesson in trying to muster up the strength to forgive like Jesus, but an assurance that—because Jesus forgave us—we *can* forgive like Him. And perhaps we will even want to.

٭٭٭٭٭٭٭

In the car on the way to my thoroughly challenging group tonight, my friend with whom I colead said, "Kelly, we can't make tonight too complicated. The most important thing these women need to know is how deeply Jesus loves them, that they're forgiven." I took my friend's timely advice and taught from Luke 7:36–50. I read the story of the woman and her alabaster jar to the three women in my group who were madder than hornets and to the one happy, happy woman in her pink sweat suit with a huge tattoo of Jesus on her leg.

(If you're familiar with this story, stroll through its offerings again. You can never know it too well.)

> Now one of the Pharisees invited Jesus to have din-
> ner with him, so he went to the Pharisee's house
> and reclined at the table. When a woman who had
> lived a sinful life in that town learned that Jesus
> was eating at the Pharisee's house, she brought an
> alabaster jar of perfume, and as she stood behind
> him at his feet weeping, she began to wet his feet

with her tears. Then she wiped them with her hair, kissed them and poured perfume on them.

When the Pharisee who had invited him saw this, he said to himself, "If this man were a prophet, he would know who is touching him and what kind of woman she is—that she is a sinner."

Jesus answered him, "Simon, I have something to tell you."

"Tell me, teacher," he said.

"Two men owed money to a certain money-lender. One owed him five hundred denarii, and the other fifty. Neither of them had the money to pay him back, so he canceled the debts of both. Now which of them will love him more?"

Simon replied, "I suppose the one who had the bigger debt canceled."

"You have judged correctly," Jesus said.

Then he turned toward the woman and said to Simon, "Do you see this woman? I came into your house. You did not give me any water for my feet, but she wet my feet with her tears and wiped them with her hair. You did not give me a kiss, but this woman, from the time I entered, has not stopped kissing my feet. You did not put oil on my head, but she has poured perfume on my feet. Therefore, I tell you, her many sins have been forgiven—for she loved much. But he who has been forgiven little loves little."

Then Jesus said to her, "Your sins are forgiven."

The other guests began to say among themselves, "Who is this who even forgives sins?"

Jesus said to the woman, "Your faith has saved you; go in peace."

This story, as much as any other in Scripture, turns religion square on its head. The "good" Pharisee who doesn't associate with sinners, who fasts and prays in public and plays by the rules, misses the forgiveness of Jesus. But the sinful woman, who needed to be forgiven of her "many sins," discovers the forgiveness of Christ and leaves emptied of her perfume but full of the ointment of peace and salvation. The glorious good news of the gospel.

According to Matthew Henry, Jesus' words "Her many sins have been forgiven—for she loved much" should be rendered, "Therefore she loved much; for it is plain, by the tenor of Christ's discourse, that the loving much was not the cause, but the effect, of her pardon." If we haven't been forgiven by Jesus, we will not know how to truly love. Or how to truly forgive.

.ʌʌʌʌʌʌʌʌʌʌʌ.

Many years ago the Lord whipped up the perfect storm of offense in my life. Please don't read too much into any particular theology here: I just know for certain that in the middle of my own sin, people's free will to hurt me, and my need to walk out forgiveness, God brewed this one up like a tornado blazing through the flatlands of Kansas. My flesh was the little house in its path, blown to bits by its twisting winds.

I was in the middle of losing a friendship deeply valuable to me, the kind of loss that happens slowly, the kind where your heart erodes one chamber at a time. I found this measure of sadness more than sufficient, not prepared for what I would feel when another person began to tear away the last vestiges of relationship I still had left with my friend. I was praying that someone would help me save my friendship, not rip it away. I found myself in a maze of pain and confusion I had no roadmap for.

Early on, it became clear that I had two options: Walk out forgiveness toward the person who had a hand in upending one of my closest friendships; or allow bitterness, jealousy, and anger to consume me. Neither felt particularly welcoming. Where was the fire hydrant of forgiveness when I needed it? I later realized that it was ever present, poised, and primed, but I was going to have to learn how to use it. Forgiveness is not the kind of thing with which you can turn the nozzle on and start blasting people. Hence, one of the greatest lessons of my life.

While trying my Sunday school hardest to extend forgiveness in practical and specific ways, I realized that even my kindness toward this person was murky at best, muddied by my own pride and need to come off as gracious. Despite my often mixed and sullied motives, I kept attempting to respond with generosity and grace, but inside I was devastated and hurt, and had no idea how to get my heart onboard with God's. I was officially out of my league in the forgiveness department, a peewee player up to bat in Fenway Park.

I won't soon forget the words the Lord spoke in my heart in response: *I want you to do this because I am a forgiving God.* This sounded so simple, almost offensively trite, but I caught something much deeper.

After all my years of knowing Jesus, I suddenly had this revelation that He wanted me to forgive this person because He wanted me to know who He is—a God of forgiveness. In other words, He wanted me to understand how much He had forgiven me, and the only way I could grasp even the tiniest crumb of this was by walking out, what felt like, impossible forgiveness in the face of deep woundedness.

Yes, I knew that Jesus had died on the cross for the world and for me and that He'd forgiven me of my sins. But when He asked me to demonstrate the nuances of forgiveness, I felt like He was saying, "Kelly, when you start forgiving, you will be more convinced of My forgiveness for you."

I suppose it's like this: The more He asked me to forgive, the more I understood His forgiveness. He wouldn't ask me to be something He Himself is not.

When the person I was striving to forgive became ill, I had the opportunity to express the intricacies of forgiveness in tangible ways. And each time I acted in forgiveness, I found out something about God that I hadn't internalized before. Every note I sent reminded me that He speaks lovingly to me even in my defiance of Him. Every colorful and fragrant flower I gave, I discovered that God blesses me with beauty despite my offenses. And with a significant gift I left, I discovered something else about Him: He lavishly blesses me, despite my many sins, despite that I've manipulated and bullied and demanded my way in the face of His love.

∿∿∿∿∿∿∿

After many months, even over a year of walking the tightrope of forgiveness, the greatest treasure I walked away with wasn't even learning to forgive, but understanding how God is a forgiving God.

I had known this on the broad scale of salvation, but now I could receive it on an emotional heart level. In places I'd never known before. This agonizing season helped me see more of the specifics of God's forgiveness toward me. Like taking apart an old transistor radio, suddenly it wasn't just one thing: forgiveness. It was a host of attitudes and attributes and actions that all connected together to make up this complex virtue.

The real revelation of this trying season wasn't the sin of the other person but the sin in my own heart. The main reason Simon the Pharisee couldn't understand why Jesus forgave that sinful woman's sin (or even had the power to forgive her) was because he was totally unaware of his own sin, his own need for forgiveness. Apart from this forgiveness there was no way he was ever going to grasp Jesus delighting in an infamously sinful woman's act of kissing Him or wetting His feet with her tears. He was never going to get the "wasted" perfume.

Simon viewed himself as righteous apart from God, fully okay on his own. Which is why the story Jesus presented to him was especially brilliant, because He went ahead and threw Simon the bone of his "good" life. Or at least his seemingly better life.

Jesus allowed Simon to identify himself with the guy who owed only fifty denarii, while the sinful woman owed five hundred. Of course this was just an illustration, as sins aren't counted in currency.

But for a moment Jesus let Simon see himself as the "better" guy (the guy with the smaller debt). The problem, which Jesus pointed out, is that if you don't have so much as a penny to your name, it doesn't matter if you owe a dime or the current national debt. If you have no way to pay, both a pack of gum and a shiny red sailboat become equally out of reach.

I had gotten really caught up in the mound of "cash" the person who hurt me owed. Her debt seemed a lot bigger than mine. I wanted God to see that I had been the good Pharisee, the one who had invited Him to dinner, put out my best china, and dimmed the sconces. I wanted Him to bless me by restoring my friendship and to reward me for how hard I had tried to love this difficult person.

It just blew my mind that while I was losing my dearest friend, and doing all I knew how to love, God seemed to be on standby. He didn't seem to be doing anything. Worse yet, He was asking me to forgive almost invisibly with no attention or fanfare. At least allow me to be celebrated for my superhuman acts of kindness and humility! (One tends to lose her spiritual mind in these cases.)

By the incredible grace of God—the grace that did not give in to my desperate fancies—He allowed me to see my fifty denarii. And that fifty was no longer four hundred fifty less than five hundred but an incalculable debt that had once separated me from the love of God.

In the face of my own sins of jealousy, control, and obsession, Jesus was allowing me to see my debt more clearly. I realized it wasn't really less than the person's who had hurt me, because the truth is that neither of us had a nickel to pay with. Apart from Jesus, we were both equally bankrupt.

When Jesus asked Simon who would love the moneylender who canceled both debts more, Simon answered correctly, "I suppose the one who had the bigger debt canceled." Jesus then turned to the woman and began to point out the striking differences between her and Simon. She had wet Jesus' feet with her tears; Simon hadn't even offered Him a bowl of water. She hadn't stopped kissing Jesus since He entered; Simon didn't once kiss the Lord. She poured out her valuable perfume on the feet of Christ; Simon didn't even anoint His head with oil.

Simon didn't love the Lord because he'd never let God forgive him. He saw no need for it. And maybe we're not like Simon in dismissing the forgiveness of Jesus for our salvation, but perhaps we are more like him than we think.

Just as Simon wondered in the privacy (or what he thought was privacy) of his mind why Jesus would allow a notoriously sinful woman to touch Him, so I was focused on the sin of this other person. There was no space for me to love Jesus by pouring out my alabaster jar or worshipping Him with my service as long as all of my attention was on someone else's sin.

But when God began to ask me to walk in forgiveness toward this person, everything changed. Not only did I learn more of the truly kind and patient forgiveness of Jesus toward me, but my heart grew more thankful for His incredible love.

I don't think I'll ever be able to fully explain what transpired inside me over that intensely painful season. Some of it will always be a mystery, the supernatural working of God that can't be described or quantified. But one thing I do know: When I released this person of her debt, I was pouring out my most precious perfume on none other than the feet of Jesus.

Those who have been forgiven much, love much.

Yes, You Really Can
Forgiveness, Part 2

C. S. Lewis once said, "Every one says forgiveness is a lovely idea, until they have something to forgive."

Forgiveness is rarely a clear path. It seems when we're on it, we're wading through the dense fog, hoping not to miss any rickety bridges over our rushing anguish, trying to avoid being tripped up by all those twisting roots of bitterness. It can be a few staggering steps forward and a couple of bruising falls backward, but I don't think it ever feels terribly straight, narrow, or flat with mild temperatures. It's a journey to be certain, the length depending much upon how deep the wound or offense and how willing we are to submit ourselves to God's process. Dying to self cannot be avoided. And yet it is strangely in this dying that we find true peace.

Perhaps this is why I am deeply moved by Jesus' parting words to the sinful woman in Luke 7: "Your sins are forgiven…. Go in peace." I think I've always known this subconsciously, but here the concept really comes to the forefront: Forgiveness and peace are great buddies. At least in my experience, if forgiveness is about anything, it's about restoring peace to an otherwise turbulent soul. And this is true whether we are receiving it or extending it. For if we haven't received God's forgiveness, we are weighed down by guilt and fear, and if we haven't extended it, we are assaulted with anger and the agonizing need to get even. I have tossed many a night this way.

As much as I desire to let forgiveness, and therefore peace, reign in my heart, I have stumbled over many stones in its pathway. Two of these stones are misunderstanding what forgiveness is or clutching my anger because it feels like the safest form of protection from being hurt again. I'm sure there are many other hindrances, but the ones I want to address in this chapter are those I've found the most challenging.

We've already looked at the biggest obstacle in the previous chapter, which is that of not accepting the forgiveness of Christ. And not just for salvation or eternal life, but also for anything we deem greater than God's grace, anything we reckon unforgivable. If we don't begin with our own need for forgiveness, we will never have the capacity to forgive others. In reality, rejecting the forgiveness of Jesus is more than an obstacle; it's a refusal that hinders us from even getting on the path of forgiving others in the first place.

I know a really brilliant, scholarly-type woman in my church who wears her hair in sophisticated, tidy buns or under hats that are often bright red. She's well traveled and married to an anesthetist. I love when *these* kinds of women have enormous passion for Scripture. They're so intriguing to me. She was teaching a six-week Bible study on forgiveness, all of which I hated to miss, but when hearing about her opening talk on Isaiah's encounter with the Lord on His throne, my only thought was, *Of course Joyce would start her teaching on forgiveness this way—she would never enter through the front door.*

Her purpose was to get her students to understand their innate sinfulness before ever even starting the process of forgiving others. She wanted them (us) to begin from the platform of "Woe to me! … I am ruined! For I am a [woman] of unclean lips, and I live among a people of unclean lips" (Isa. 6:5). The class was equally grateful and stunned by her opening talk, because I think most everyone who files into a class about forgiveness does so carrying a well-worn suitcase holding their biggest grievances. We're interested in learning how to sort through the soiled offenses we've been toting around so we can ultimately let go of them through forgiveness. This is good but still centered on the wrongs others have caused us. Not too many people come in thinking, *I wonder how many people are carrying around suitcases packed with wounds I've inflicted; I wonder what it cost God to forgive me.* But this is precisely where Joyce wanted her class to begin.

Because those who love much know they have been forgiven much.

〜〜〜〜〜〜〜

C. S. Lewis wrote this about forgiveness in *Mere Christianity*: "A good many people imagine that forgiving your enemies means making out that they are really not such bad fellows after all, when it is quite plain that they are."[1] When faced with having to let people off the hook, so to speak, we can easily become terrified by the notion that if we release our offenders from their debt toward us, we will in essence be saying that what they did wasn't wrong. Or that they are good people, when both may not be true at all. This false idea has kept so many of us, myself included, from extending true forgiveness, because we just can't bear the thought of glossing over the deep wounds someone has inflicted on us as though those wounds never existed.

But forgiveness is not denying what our enemies have done; it's not calling something whole that's fractured or something pure that's corroded. Forgiveness is looking in the face of what our offenders have done, recognizing their wound for all that it is, and then choosing to forgive. Still. It has nothing to do with denying the wrong of those who hurt us but has everything to do with changing our hearts toward them: No more offering up every ounce of our unoccupied thinking space for dreaming about their demise. No more secretly finding joy in hearing that they lost their job or got tossed by their boyfriend or have a crippling illness. Forgiveness means laying down our sword of vengeance. Even praying God's blessing upon the person who hurt us can be one of the most powerful balms to our souls. I know what you're thinking: *Kelly, one impossible step at a time.*

That said, there are definitely instances where punishment or consequences must still be implemented (sometimes by the person who has been wronged), but only for the good of the offender and for the sake of justice. Forgiveness is not in opposition to justice or consequences, but it is certainly at odds with hate and revenge. It's all a matter of how our hearts frame our enemies. If we find ourselves glorying in their destruction, chances are we haven't quite reached the core of forgiveness. Yet.

∿∿∿∿∿∿∿

I was making a homemade pasta sauce out of vine-ripened cherry tomatoes, fresh garlic, and zucchini on Valentine's Day, or Galentine's Day as my friend Paige likes to refer to it. (Horrifically cheesy, I know, but strangely comforting to be able to reclaim the day for the singles of my gender.) The recipe called for fresh or canned artichoke hearts, but some silent alarm of compromise sounded at the thought of buying something canned for my otherwise from-scratch meal. I knew that none of my dinner guests would know if I cut a canned artichoke corner here or there, but I figured if I was going to the trouble of rolling out homemade semolina pasta dough, I would learn how to cut a fresh artichoke in a way that laid bare its prized heart.

This was possibly one of the greatest errors of my young-adult life. After whittling away the pointy leaves of four artichokes, I think I came away with enough quartered hearts for one guest to have one sliver in one bite. Before sautéing these little remnants, I treasured them in a bowl of lemon juice like they were on the endangered species list, because—who knew—artichoke hearts oxidize immediately. I don't think I've ever coddled a food more, perhaps besides pine nuts, which can cost you a day's wage if you overbroil them.

Eventually I decided to "supplement" with the silly cans.

But for all my defeat, I found scraping the furry little choke out of the center of the heart soothingly therapeutic. This may reveal that I need other forms of therapy, but at the very least I liked the image of ridding a valuable delicacy of its thistly center. Forgiveness can be much the same way: Often it involves a lot of peeling away of layers. We find ourselves rejoicing over one discarded leaf of bitterness here and another leaf of anger there, while still recognizing we have a few more of revenge and gossip to go. If we're intent on seeking the Bible for its healing truths, we'll find it as smart as a paring knife, sharp enough to discern the motives and desires of our hearts. Which is essential when walking through forgiveness.

If you will indulge me with the artichoke analogy for one more paragraph (I'm really trying to get my wasted-artichoke money's worth), it has been my experience that even after shedding my bitter leaves, the whole thing eventually comes down to one prickly center: the core of the wound. It might be rejection, abandonment, betrayal, slander, loss of innocence; but whatever it is, you will always know it. It will be the ugliest and most difficult piece to reconcile, and it will be the last thing to stand between you and the glory of a cleansed heart. It will take the grace of God to scrape the thing out, but it will be worth every supernatural release if you allow Him to do it—and you can take that straight to the lemon juice bowl. (I just went too far, didn't I?)

Still, when we're faced with the deepest betrayals of life, such as affairs, the losses from a divorce, childhood abuse, or a drunk driver who killed a loved one, just the idea of forgiveness can seem like a reckless invitation to throw our very last vestige of control out the window. In our most painful circumstances, unforgiveness seems like the one thing we still have left!

When I sat with my Bible study group for women in recovery one night, it was clear that, whether they knew it or not, holding on to unforgiveness was a matter of control for them. They walked in the door, complaining about how everyone had wronged them, how the whole system was out to get them. They declared they weren't going to take it anymore, no one was going to tell them what to do, and anyone who tried was going to pay. These collective thoughts, though bristling to me, were comforting to them. Anger and revenge had become their security blankets; they clutched unforgiveness like a well-worn teddy bear. In their minds, to forgive was to give up their protection. And isn't this exactly how we have all felt at certain times when faced with having to forgive, especially those who have hurt us the deepest?

So what do we do with the idea that forgiveness threatens our control? Is forgiveness—even for the worst of offenses—truly synonymous with losing our grip on things? I know when I was working through forgiveness toward the person who tore my friend away, forgiving meant letting go, and yes, letting go meant losing control. But losing control to whom? To the friend who manipulated and hurt me, or to the God who loves me and cares a great deal about justice? I believe that forgiveness *does* mean losing control, not to the reckless offender but rather to the capable heart of God. "So then, those who suffer according to God's will should commit themselves to *their faithful Creator* and continue to do good" (1 Peter 4:19).

Letting go of our control and placing it in God's hands is not easy, because being out of control is precisely the condition we were in when the abuse took place, the affair happened, the undeserved lawsuit came down, our best friend betrayed us, we were sold to Midianite merchants.... The story of Joseph (found in the later chapters of Genesis) gives us a penetrating picture of being hurt and out of control. I'm not sure there is a better story in the entire Bible that speaks not only to forgiveness but also to God's purposeful hand in the midst of injustice.

vvvvvvvvvvv

Sparsely sketched, Joseph was the son of Jacob and Rachel, born into a prominent family. He had ten half brothers, sons of Jacob's wife Leah, and one full brother, who was born to Jacob's other wife, Rachel. The sons of Leah were insanely jealous of Joseph, mostly because he was the prize of his father's eye and had dreamed that his brothers would one day bow down to him. Though his dreams were legitimate, he would have done better to have managed a little more like Mary, pondering it all in her heart instead of flaunting how great he would one day be. Joseph's proclamation of his dreams incensed his brothers so much that they plotted to kill him by leaving him for dead in a pit. That was until they stood to profit by dragging him out of the pit and selling him to foreigners who took him back to their land and enslaved him. (Few of us have a category for this kind of cruelty where we live, though brothels, sex trafficking, and slavery are heinous crimes that plague our world every day. This is one reason I am grateful for the Bible's honesty and detail of injustice, because it portrays real-life forgiveness in the face of real-life suffering.)

My hunch is that you've not been bound up in an Egyptian dungeon recently, but I'm confident you can relate to being hurt in a way that was out of your control, in a way you certainly didn't choose. Because this is so often the case when people hurt us, the idea of offering forgiveness belies our desire to hang on to the tiny thread of control we still have left.

But this is where reframing our fears is essential: Forgiveness is about placing the wrongs against us, not back in the hands of our enemies, but in the hands of God. Because Scripture is a running story of God working on the behalf of those who have suffered unjustly, I believe there is no safer place to be:

After Hagar's mistress, Sarai, abused her, an angel of the Lord appeared to her and said, "The LORD has *heard* of your misery" (Gen. 16:11).

After Leah was thrust upon a husband who did not love her, we read, "When the LORD *saw* that Leah was not loved, he opened her womb" (Gen. 29:31).

After Hannah wept because of her barrenness and suffered the mockery of her husband's other wife, who had many children, God turned the tables: "She who was barren has borne seven children, but she who has had many sons pines away" (1 Sam. 2:5).

The psalmist writes:

> But you, O God, do see trouble and grief;
>   you consider it to take it in hand.
> The victim commits himself to you;
>   you are the helper of the fatherless. (Ps. 10:14)

And Peter adds:

> So then, those who suffer according to God's will
> should commit themselves to their faithful Creator
> and continue to do good. (1 Peter 4:19)

"I find it very hard to generate forgiveness for anyone who has wronged me yet doesn't care, doesn't realize they have wronged me, doesn't want to (or refuses to) apologize." This was written by a woman who responded to a question I posed about forgiveness, but it might as well been penned by anyone who has made it past kindergarten. So what do you do here? How in the world do you forgive someone who isn't asking for forgiveness? This can be an enormous hang-up for those of us who have waited, even years, for someone to come back to us, hash through everything that went wrong, and end with a long, detailed apology that is preferably mingled with a lot of weeping and a couple drops of their blood. Or maybe your fantasies aren't quite as thorough as mine: You simply want someone to acknowledge that what they did was wrong and that it hurt you. But here's the question: If you never get this, can you still forgive? The resounding answer of the Bible is yes, yes, yes. Absolutely, unequivocally yes.

Yes.

Why? Because forgiveness is not at all dependent upon someone asking for it. It's not dependent upon the person acknowledging his or her wrong, or begging for mercy. Forgiveness is freestanding by its very nature. Perfectly autonomous.

~~~~~~~~~~~

Years after Joseph's brothers had sold him into slavery, he became the most powerful man in the region, second only to Pharaoh. His power was tied to the keys he owned to every grain barn in Egypt during a devastating famine. A famine that propelled his brothers out of the land of Canaan to his very feet; only his brothers didn't recognize him in the linen robe and gold chains. Perhaps the fluent Egyptian threw them as well. Once Joseph revealed himself to his brothers—and before they could even say a word—he offered, "And now, do not be distressed and do not be angry with yourselves."

Note: This was not a response to a heartfelt apology by his shady brothers for trying to ruin his life. They hadn't even pulled their thoughts together enough to speak, much less say they were sorry. No true repentance on their part is ever recorded in the story, yet Joseph was quick to relieve them of any guilt or heartache.

I can't imagine that Joseph grabbed such an immediate, forgiving response out of the thin palace air. It rolled off his tongue too easily, like he'd been rehearsing it in Hebrew for years. This unexpected and gracious reply to the brothers who had betrayed and abused him simply could not have been birthed in that single moment. Joseph had reconciled everything his brothers had done to him long before they showed up asking for grain. Perhaps he had worked it through in Potiphar's house or on the dungeon floors of his cell or while blazing through the desert sands of Egypt on his roaring chariot. Or, more realistically, perhaps in *all* of those places, working through each layer one supernatural step at a time. We're not told, but what's clear is that Joseph forgave his brothers long before he knew if he'd ever see them again. A formal apology from them was irrelevant to his being able to forgive.

〰〰〰〰〰

I have a friend who is struggling in the aftermath of a broken relationship. It's been over a year, and she's still reeling and wanting to
know why the guy who once loved her so zealously broke up with
her, why he drew her in and rolled out the red carpet, and then just
as she was getting used to its cushiness underneath her bare feet, he
reeled it back up like the best vacuum cleaner retrieves its own cord.
She had been dealt some real blows over the course of this relationship, not totally independent of her own very real issues; but still,
this guy could stand to be sorry for a sizable portion. The paralyzing
problem—at least in the eyes of my friend—is that he's not sorry, he's
not talking, and he's made it clear he never wants to see her again.

My friend and I have gone round and round on the dizzying
merry-go-round of my saying she needs to forgive him, and to release
him and those miserable years to God, and her saying that a conversation with him would miraculously fix her entire life. If he would just
say he's sorry. To which I always reply, "This may never come." I've
even gathered the boldness more recently to say, "I'm pretty sure this
almost absolutely for sure will not come," while making clear that his
apology, or lack of one, has no bearing whatsoever on whether she
can forgive him. Or whether she can experience peace and freedom
and life apart from him.

So far, my attempts to persuade her that forgiveness is not
dependent on her ex-boyfriend's understanding of his wrongdoings
have been poorly received. She's convinced that a long, drawn-out
explanation and apology from him is the answer. But she's getting
this confused with reconciliation. For a relationship to be put back
together and sewed up, you have to have the discussions and the
apologies. But you don't need to have either of these for forgiveness.

You just need God. Since it is God who commands us to forgive our enemies—and promises to mend our wounds—it is God who will help us forgive those who have trespassed against us. And right now her unforgiveness is eating her up.

But the truth is, the most elaborate apology in the world won't make the difference we spend so much precious time fantasizing about anyway. Especially if our significant hang-ups are with a parent or long-term relationship, we can find ourselves just as easily thinking something along the lines of, *Oh, so now that you're ready to say you're sorry, I'm just supposed to sweep the last twenty years under the carpet?* Not to mention that most broken relationships are so complex it would take the FBI and the next few lifetimes to get to the bottom of who wronged who and why. As my dad likes to say, "It's similar to showing up to the scene of a house that's just burnt straight to the ground and then being asked to find the match that started the fire."

For those who are desperate for freedom from tumultuous angst, I'll deliver it in one more way: You don't have to be able to find the match to forgive. You don't need an apology. You don't need the other person to say he or she is sorry. You don't even need the person to be aware of the pain he or she has caused you. The person could even be dead. You can still forgive. *You really can.*

◦◦◦◦◦◦◦◦◦◦◦

While going through the long, agonizing struggle of losing one of my dearest friendships and while dealing with the person who couldn't seem happier to watch the whole thing dissolve, I kept hearing the oddest phrase roll through my mind—the kind of phrase you don't hear with your actual ears but with whatever ones are in your soul. It was an astonishing message: *Take this as from My hand.* I gathered this voice was the Lord's, mostly because He's the only one who tends to speak to me silently and with such paucity of words, never long-winded, just supremely impacting. I heard this phrase while nursing my pain on a quiet walk along a winding creek at the bottom of what I would like to say was a mountain, but in reality we only have hills in Nashville. I heard these same words when I had the wind knocked out of me at a social gathering where I was not entirely ignored but just a smidge short of that, which left me more like *tolerated.* This kind of distance coming from a once-intimate group of friends devastated me.

Take this as from My hand. It was the same message for months and months—it was like having a friend traveling through Europe who keeps sending you different postcards from Paris and Milan and Geneva, all with the same message. But I understood why I needed to hear this one over and over. I would have to choose to believe that all the pain of this loss was from the hand of a person yet, mysteriously, straight from the hand of God.

Now please don't ask me to try to explain whether or not God allows evil or ordains it, or if sin is a matter of free will or God's providence, or from where evil originated. My mind just can't stretch to those places, and the scholars whose minds can usually disagree, so don't get hung up there in the outer stratosphere or you might miss the person you're supposed to forgive for all the theology. Here is what I know: God is sovereign. When His gentle voice told me to take the painful circumstances as coming from His very hand, it allowed me to view the loss from a different perspective. When the lonely moments stranded me cold and afraid and the sometimes-cruel ones left me writhing, I had a firm sense that all this suffering wasn't random. I had an understanding that God was rooting the wickedness out of my own heart and that He was yanking some monstrous idols out of there while He was at it. But even beyond personal holiness, I had a palpable sense that God was protecting me from some relationships that ultimately were not the best for me. I had the kind of faith that alternately believed and had not a skosh of hope that He had other people for me down the road who would love me more wholly.

～～～～～～～

After Joseph endured betrayal by his brothers, the loss of countless years with his family that could never be returned, a false accusation from a woman who accused him of rape, and several years in Pharaoh's prison, he said the most remarkable thing to the brothers who had stolen what we would consider his very life: *What you meant for evil, God meant for good* (Gen. 50:20). It is incumbent upon us to pause here. We must allow these words to ring out into the most distant caverns of our souls. Could it really be that God is gathering all the years of wrongdoing to your soul, harvesting it for an unimaginable feast He is preparing, and spreading it on a table He is setting? And not just for heaven, but for some very tangible realities here on earth? Just a thought. Or more accurately, a truth for those who are willing to trust their souls to a faithful Creator.

Perhaps you're thinking this was a one-off deal for Joseph, but that would be to exclude many other biblical accounts, the message of Romans 8:28, and God's very nature. He is a master at taking what people meant for our harm and reworking it for our good. This is what He *does*. We see this also illustrated earlier in Joseph's story when he said to his brothers, "Do not be angry with yourselves for selling me here, because it was to save lives that God sent me ahead of you" (Gen. 45:5). Joseph's brothers *sold* him, but God *sent* him. How can both of these be true? Such mysteries can be understood only within the sovereignty of God.

Having a redeeming view of God's sovereignty greatly helps us reframe the wounds inflicted upon us by our enemies. Throughout Joseph's story we see him referencing the many ways that God used the evil of his brothers to save and preserve the lives of a mighty remnant. God lavished Joseph with blessings that far exceeded anything he could have dreamed of as a little boy in Canaan. And as the narrator of Genesis tells us over and over, God was with Joseph, whether in the palace or in the prison. He was present when his brothers mocked him, when his coat was stripped, when he was sold to merchants. He was present when someone lied about him and someone else forgot him. God never left him. And He has never left us.

Let us clear forgiveness's path of its most daunting, looming obstacles. We must start with our own sin. "Woe is me!" is a really good place to begin before God. Once we've established our own need for forgiveness, we need not fear that forgiving our enemies means losing control to them—only to God, and in this case, we can rest confidently in His ever-capable and just hands. And if this is still at all fuzzy, we positively do not need those who have hurt us to admit they're wrong. If this admission comes, it is delicious icing, but not at all necessary for offering forgiveness. And lastly, let us lighten our dim view of God's sovereignty, realizing anew that He is the One who can restore the years the locusts have eaten (Joel 2:25). Realizing that He can turn our deepest heartaches into unthinkable blessings. It is here that Joseph's words bear repeating, "What you intended for evil, God intended for good."

Forgive. Peace is waiting....

Not as the World Gives

Peace, Part 1

Peace is often thought of as serene and billowy, a languid train winding through the countryside of our surroundings, leaving calm in its wake. I love it when I hear this particular horn signaling from a distance, because there's nothing wrong with a good old English understanding of the quieting word *peace*.

I just attended my first-ever princess birthday party for my six-year-old friend, Mary Holland, where eleven little girls ate fancy cake and sipped pink lemonade out of flowery teacups, all of them dressed up as princesses. I ended up functioning as the resident fingernail painter, which is a real stretch for those who know me; though each little princess thought her nails were *simply mahvelous* after visiting my salon. Lots of squealing and giggling and the highest concentration of pink I may have ever seen in one room filled the space. As the party wound down, and each little sugar-spiked princess bounded to her car in her featherweight slippers, I could sense a measure of peace being restored to the house one little princess's exit at a time. One of my adult friends, who was *not* dressed up as a princess, asked me how quickly I'd be on the couch with a warm beverage in my hand and a candle flickering on the coffee table. I was already holding the lighter.

Although peace can definitely overlap rest and serenity, there is more to the biblical sense of the word. While individual, soulful, and serene, peace is an essential part of God's design for us, it doesn't completely represent *shalom* or *eirene* (the Hebrew and Greek words for *peace* respectively) in their entirety. Peace can also be strong and tenacious, bringing restoration to relationships that at one point held less hope for wholeness than a shattered mirror could ever wish to offer a reflection. Paul says in Romans 16:20, "The God of peace will soon crush Satan under your feet." Interesting how peace and destruction are linked here. Jesus was prophesied in Isaiah as the Prince of Peace, but He could overturn weighty tables of greed and knew how to valiantly defend vulnerable women against the self-righteous, piercing accusations of the Pharisees. He came to restore brokenness and bring crushed hearts to wholeness. Peace is not always tame.

Because of the multifaceted nature of peace and the many streams of definitions from which we come to understand it, peace can be a difficult notion to grasp. In our culture we hear loose ideas concocted from church, Oprah, best friends, movie stars, St. John's Wort, with a few Bible verses shaken in like red pepper flakes for spiritual flavor. We may define *peace* as the feeling we have after a moving worship service, a trip to the yoga studio, an evening rocking a sleeping newborn, a healing conversation, tumbling into bed after an exhausting day, an afternoon of reading on the beach, or after our house has just been cleaned. *Peace!*

But what is it actually?

The Hebrew word for peace, *shalom*, means "completeness, wholeness, health, peace, welfare, safety, soundness, tranquility, prosperity, perfectness, fullness, rest, harmony, and the absence of agitation or discord."[1] *Shalom* is meant to bring us peace with God, with ourselves, and with others—so much as this third one lies with us. It is multidimensional not just in the ways it affects our relationship with God, self, and people but also in the dynamic forms in which it expresses itself. However, most of the time I meet people who are looking for an individual sense of peace—the deep inner kind that governs our hearts and souls even in the midst of difficult circumstances.

Though inner harmony and feelings of tranquility don't entirely sum up the biblical definition of peace, they are often the elements of rest that we most urgently sense are missing. This is especially true in our harried Western culture where many are simmering with anxiety, glued to their phones, unrested, disquieted, riding the waves of their fears, longing to lose the nagging doubts and mistrust that do nothing but haunt and hover. They are looking for the soul rest that seems to accompany the candle and the couch—at least whatever this looks like on a heart level. Most of us are desperate for a quieter life, free from the cacophony of the world and our minds. But to get to this inner peace—the kind most of us mean when we say we need more "peace"—we must first have a foundation for it.

〰〰〰〰〰〰〰

I recently skimmed a book written by a truly exquisite writer who traveled the world looking for a Zen-like harmonious peace, receiving a generous enough advance from her publisher to pay for the whole excursion. (I am still holding out for a similar offer: *How Kelly Discovered the Virtues in All Her Favorite European Cities over Delicately Prepared Cuisine*, or something like that.) This author is bright and strings words together with a needle of brilliance and a thread of eloquence, but though I appreciate her writing style, she has stitched together a worldview of peace entirely different from my most foundational beliefs. Early in her book she writes, "I can't swallow that one fixed rule of Christianity insisting that Christ is the *only* path to God."[2]

It is ironic that this exact fixed "rule" is the basis for all peace I have in my life: Jesus Christ. If He is not the only path to God, then as a Christian I have no basis for peace whatsoever, because my entire life, the forgiveness of my sin, and all my future hope hang upon the thread of this one truth. ("If *only* for this life we have hope in Christ, we are to be pitied more than all men," writes Paul in 1 Corinthians 15:19.) I think this is why Paul so often addressed his letters with the phrase "Grace and peace to you from God our Father and *the Lord Jesus Christ*." Because peace cannot be separated from Jesus, and peace can exist only *after* grace. There is no peace if there is not first grace, because it is through this grace we are forgiven and can have a secure relationship with God, and that relationship brings peace to our restless souls.

So many have taken issue with the seeming exclusivity of Christianity, a belief this author can't begin to "swallow." (Timothy Keller, in his book *Reason for God*, does a remarkable job of treating the idea that *every* belief system is an exclusive one.) Yet it is this very claim of Jesus—"I am the way and the truth and the life. No one comes to the Father except through me" (John 14:6)—that offers us peace, because although the Person through whom salvation comes is singular, He is anything but exclusive, offering peace with God to those who desire Him from any race, gender, or culture, rich or poor.

Though Christ as the only way to God will indeed be hard to swallow for some, I wholeheartedly believe we must begin here, our only hope for true peace. Paul writes in Romans 5:1, "Therefore, since we have been justified through faith, we have *peace* with God through our Lord Jesus Christ." We've already addressed the idea of justification, but it bears repeating that since God sees Jesus' righteousness when He looks upon His children, we have peace with Him. Peace with God means we have a restored relationship with Him, intimacy unbroken by sin. When Jesus takes that sin away, peace is given.

‧‧‧‧‧‧‧‧‧

This morning I found myself relieved to be sitting under the zealous shears of my hairdresser, Ben, because my hair had gotten disastrously long and free-spirited. He's a creative sort of stylist who made his own leather pouch for his scissors and grooming supplies, all decked out with bronze crosses and studs. I found out today that he is marginally Catholic; and when I say marginally, I mean it is the religion he most identifies himself with, given his upbringing and his Irish and French-Canadian roots, but I'm not sure how much he actually practices his faith. He seems to have an appreciation for

God and the constructs of the church, but I don't get the impression he attends Mass very often. He's a hockey-playing, beer-drinking, really nice guy who can cut hair with precision and surety; however, the afterlife is vague to him. As we chatted about God and religion, he quipped with a hint of weighty seriousness, "If Saint Peter doesn't have a sense of humor, I'm in big trouble."

I get the sense that Ben's hoping to wiggle into heaven based on being an overall good guy, despite being a little edgy and wayward at times, stuff he's hoping someone like Peter will turn a blind eye to if this saint doesn't find his misgivings a little funny after all. As I listened to Ben, I wanted to talk more about the grace I see in the Bible—the grace that doesn't need to look the other way because it wholly forgives—but the blow-dryer was a bit loud for this. I could have yelled Ephesians 2:8–9 across the salon, but I can't say this is especially my style of evangelism before noon. At least I was able to describe the fabulousness of how my home church celebrates grace while hopefully saying enough to keep the conversation going the next time my hair starts to overtake my personal space (not that I was trying to talk him out of his church—as the gospel can be missed in any denomination—but perhaps into an additional perspective of grace).

More than anything, I was struck by the lack of peace Ben's uncertain belief system must provoke in him, not knowing if he'll make it into purgatory, heaven, neither, and what the criteria is for entrance, not to mention who will be laying down the gavel—be it Jesus, Peter, or someone else. It would be hard not knowing which way the scales were going to tip after living your life to the best of your ability while still knowing your darker moments would require a saint to give you a wink and a fist bump, like, *You and me, buddy, we're cool … come on in.* John Stott said, "The gospel is good news of mercy to the undeserving. The symbol of the religion of Jesus is the cross, not the scales."[3] It is my prayer that Ben finds peace in the cross, because the unforgiving scales that weigh good deeds versus bad have left him uneasy—as they would any of us.

〰〰〰〰〰〰

Just as the cross offers us peace with God, it also offers us peace with others, one of my favorite by-products of the Christian faith. The Bible brims with secrets of peacemaking, and I refer to them as secrets because they're different from what we tend to get most anywhere else: God's counsel offers peace through the unexpected avenues of forgiveness, praying for those who accuse and hurt us, exuding patience with those who tug at our serenity. His words instruct us that peace is often restored when we humble ourselves in our relationships and own our wrongs, even if our percentage of wrong is somewhere in the less-than-50-percent category, a point that we have marked out with precision. The Bible says crazy things like *love covers a multitude of sins* and *a soft answer turns away wrath* and *don't repeat a matter because it separates friends.* All this for the sake of peace.

These are "crazy," because most of us find it more reasonable to highlight other people's sins and return wrath with a slice of revenge and rehearse all the burning tidbits of gossip that traveled through our hearing earlier that day. But peace with others—well, we never get peace with others this way. We may get even, but we don't get peace. Which is why the Bible is essential to our understanding of peace with others, because it offers us revelation on the subject that we wouldn't otherwise know.

The peace that Jesus preached is about having access to God our Father through Him, and therefore gaining a new power to be at peace with others insofar as it lies with us. This is why Paul urges us to make *every effort* to live at peace with one another, and though we often think of peace as being the absence of exertion, the making of it can be downright toilsome. Peace has to be fought for, especially when hurt feelings and wrongs are barring its way. It may require the hard work of giving forgiveness, or the seeking of it, depending on which side of the offense you're on. However, our efforts will never outweigh the joy of peace restored to souls who were once at odds (Eph. 2:17–18).

Jesus is the premise for the peace for which we long, and He offers Himself to the most religious as well as to the puck-stick-and-beer-loving hairdresser who is really "hoping" to get in. Peace comes through knowing, and knowing comes not from the possible good graces of St. Peter or our best stab at being "good" but through the blood of Jesus. John says, "I write these things to you who believe in the name of the Son of God so that you may *know* that you have eternal life" (1 John 5:13).

ᴡᴡᴡᴡᴡᴡᴡᴡ

Shortly after Jesus explained to His disciples that He is the exclusive way to God, He said, "Peace I leave with you; my peace I give you. *I do not give to you as the world gives*" (John 14:27). This is a wonderful distinction, because even the most well-meaning parents, world leaders, spouses, or friends ultimately do not have the power to offer us unshakable peace. When presidents are elected into office, they promise to defend our peace, but just when we think we are virtually invincible, a fleet bombs Pearl Harbor or two planes slam into the World Trade Center.

My parents did everything in their power to structure a safe life of peace for me, but still the monsters under the bed and threats of tornadoes and doubts about my faith slid through the cracks of the fortress they had created. The "world" gives peace only in the way that it can give, which is always prone to punctures.

I remember attending a women's event in Europe when a great deal of fear began to churn inside my chest like a mini-cyclone. My trip coincided with a tremendous financial collapse in the United States that set off tremors throughout the rest of the world. At the same time, a terrorist bomb went off in a hotel several countries away from where I was staying in England, but I was still a few thousand miles closer to the explosion than if I had been at home in Nashville. The British newscasters who were reporting all this didn't try to warm my heart any, by the way. There's no rush on their part to offer consolation; just the cool flair of their accents letting you know how terrified we should all be.

Simultaneously, my best friend was in a dangerous part of Africa working on a project regarding the AIDS pandemic, and we had terrible times trying to connect over time zones and spotty cell coverage that was more mottled than the back roads she was on in Uganda. I was nearing the brink of full-throttle anxiety when another close friend called to tell me of unexplainable gas shortages in Nashville causing lines of cars to wrap around buildings and down interstates. I never thought I'd have this thought as a born-and-raised northern

Virginia girl, but I longed for my pillow and a Southern accent. I wanted someone to hold me and say, "Bless your heart," whether they meant it or not. I found myself scrambling for peace. I prayed a lot.

Our peace is easily disrupted in this world, regardless of whether it is trivial frustrations or more seriously agitating experiences that ruffle our solace. This morning I had a business situation that sent me reeling. I was so riled up I had to call a friend, looking for comfort and reassurance (peace), but since she was in the middle of a meeting, she asked if I could take a walk around the block to gather myself until she could call me back. "No!" I said. "I don't have time to walk around the block. I have to finish this chapter on *peace!*"

Only God could effectively restore the peace I needed in this situation, and He gives it not as the world does. In my friend's absence, He spoke to me through passages of Scriptures, gently reminding me of His able hands when it seemed like so many important pieces were being misplaced. He challenged me with the need for humility, as it's easy to trot high on your horse when you think you're right and everyone else is so clearly wrong in their fancy suits. I have found that authentic peace follows the voice of God. The presence of His voice and the content of His words give us peace, but we have to listen. And sometimes this means putting down the phone, closing the computer, or flicking off any number of distractions.

It was through all of these loving reminders from God and His Word that peace was restored to me today, a peace with more staying power than even my best friend could have offered if she hadn't been stuck in a meeting. (I may have gotten understanding from her, a person on my "side," but probably not lasting peace.) As Charles Spurgeon put it:

> Furthermore, even when the world's wishes of peace are sincere, what are they but *mere wishes....* Now, not so, does Christ give. If he says "Peace be with you," his benediction is most true and full of sweet sincerity. He left his own peace in heaven, that he might give the peace which he enjoyed with his Father, to us in this world of sorrow, for thus he puts it, "My peace I give unto you." Christ, when he blesses, blesses not in word only, but in deed. The lips of truth cannot promise more than the hands of love will surely give.[4]

When waves of disruption play havoc with our lives, only God can give us the deep, abiding peace that rests on the ocean floor. The problem is, most of the time we're willing to settle for a much weaker version of it. We'll drink the extra glass of wine or spend an hour of fruitless twaddle, hashing through our troubles with a friend. But all along, God wants to speak deeply to what is troubling us and desires to give us a peace that is different from the paper-thin comforts of the world. But it can be a fearful thing to sit quietly before God, wondering what He will speak or *if* He will speak. Sometimes we're afraid of the voices in our own heads, the ones that condemn and chide us, and so we avoid silence, because it's not all that silent. However, this is exactly when we need to make the decision to sit with God, the One who says that He Himself is our peace. And we will know it when He gives us such peace, because it is thorough and deep and transcends our understanding and circumstances (Phil. 4:7). It is stronger than the human arms of a spouse. Far superior to the fleeting security of wealth. More assuring than our most familiar surroundings. As Spurgeon so insightfully shared, Christ does not offer us mere wishes, but He matches the promise of peace with the deeds of His loving and powerful hands. He gives not as the world gives.

/wwwwwwww

It is true that we can have this otherworldly peace only when we come to know God through Jesus Christ. However, I think it's possible to be forgiven of your sins and know that you will be with Jesus when you die, while still running around this earth like a mad woman who might just go into cardiac arrest if she has to wait in one more grocery store line run by a clerk who appears to be scanning her first-ever orange. I believe we can have eternal peace with God and still be wracked with jealousy or unable to sleep at night because of recurring fears. Our peace can be stolen by bitterness and chased away by insecurity—as in, we had peace just before the beautiful neighbor moved in next door who's a size 2. Essentially, you can't have true peace without first coming into relationship with Jesus, but I believe you *can* have a relationship with Christ without always experiencing the deep peace God intends His children to have. This has much to do with the plethora of other things that cover up the gift of inner peace, the soul rest so many of us are longing for.

I cannot tell you how many years I have lived trying to tame a swirling mind and quell a churning stomach as a result of fear, guilt, anger, or sometimes just too much coffee. I'm fundamentally wired a little tight and anxious, but I'll tell you that the vast majority of my internal unrest had little to do with my DNA and much more to do with a waning trust in God while indulging myself down paths of my own choosing. Sometimes my anxiety had to do with wounds that lie open with no balm. But no matter the source, I see from one end of Scripture to the other that God longs for His people's hearts to be at rest, even if our circumstances are far from restful. And since I feel certain I'm not the only one who has ever wrestled perpetually jostling insides while looking calm on the outside, I'll spend the next chapter reflecting on how to cultivate a heart at peace. If we have been given the miracle of peace with God and with others, most assuredly this same wonder should be rooted within ourselves.

A Soul at Rest

Peace, Part 2

"The LORD bless you and keep you; the LORD make his face shine upon you and be gracious to you; the LORD turn his face toward you and *give you peace*" (Num. 6:24–26). It is the Lord who grants us peace, a gift that comes solely from Him. This is vital to understand, because it can be more natural to think that peace rolls in when everything has lined up in our universes with calming precision—when we're healthy, happy, wealthy, whole, and everyone around us is doing exactly what we need them to. But biblical peace is far more than everything being in its place. It's a steadying anchor even in turbulent waters. I've had to adjust my thinking here over the years, recognizing that my truest peace has to do with God's presence and what He says is true about me, not so much with everything holding together just so. It has little to do with my external circumstances and everything to do with the voice and nearness of God. I can have peace amidst tumult if only I have Him.

If God's presence is the source of our peace, then His ways draw the boundaries around it. The Bible speaks a lot about the peace that accompanies a righteous life, one that is anchored in God's principles. He has given us instructions that encircle a life of peace, like a sturdy fence surrounding its property. However, we sometimes see God's prescriptions for our lives as confining, not sources of blessing and freedom. Yet the by-product of holy living is inner peace, something the Bible often attests to: "Now then, my sons, listen to me; blessed are those who keep my ways" (Prov. 8:32). Wisdom's "ways are pleasant ways, and all her paths are peace" (Prov. 3:17). The psalmist proclaims, "Blessed are they whose ways are blameless, who walk according to the law of the LORD. Blessed are they who keep his statutes and seek him with all their heart" (Ps. 119:1–2).

〰〰〰〰

I was reading that often-quoted passage in Philippians 4 the other morning: "Whatever is true, whatever is noble, whatever is right, whatever is pure, whatever is lovely, whatever is admirable—if anything is excellent or praiseworthy—think about such things." I noticed that peace is the culmination of these words found in the following verse: "Whatever you have learned or received or heard from me, or seen in me—*put it into practice. And the God of peace will be with you.*" I saw in this passage how essential living by God's commands is to a life of peace. Paul encourages the Philippians to learn, receive, hear, see, and most poignant, put into practice the truths and lifestyle he lived as a result of Jesus Christ: a way of life that promotes inward peace.

We can whimsically recite these sentiments of all that is lovely, noble, excellent, and admirable, almost getting them confused with, say, a poem about blue bonnets and rose petals. And chocolates. Yet this is a compelling charge for us to have our thoughts consumed with all that is right and true, an unspoken call for us to lay aside whatever is not of those things. I have a dear pastor friend who leads a church in southern Florida and is vigilant about what passes across his computer and television screens, because as he so eloquently puts it, "Our vision is fragile." Indeed it is.

Paul reminds us to dwell on the excellent and praiseworthy and to practice what he so diligently lived and taught. We can know what these teachings are, along with how Paul lived, because so many of his letters are preserved for us in the New Testament. We must simply read and meditate on Scripture while adding action to our faith by practicing its teachings. And these practices do not travel alone but are accompanied by the *God of peace*. After all, peace and God's ways are the dearest of companions.

Certainly, I have forfeited this divine peace at different times in my life for the pleasures and pursuits that the world waves at me like intoxicating sparklers. I have watched others exchange such peace for the same delusions, frolicking all the way to their own heartbreak. This is why God so lovingly warns against the seductive trappings of the illicit affair, sex beyond the covenant promise of marriage (as antiquated as this sounds in our century), blurring the truth for our

gain, addicting ourselves to materialism, and a litany of other allur-
ing charms. We believe these things will bring us the satisfaction and
peace our hearts desire, but in reality we end up struggling to sleep at
night, our chests heavy, our minds racing, because we have forfeited
one of the greatest prizes of the Christian life: peace. All for the life
we insist we must live *our* way.

The great German theologian and martyr Dietrich Bonhoeffer
wisely wrote in *The Cost of Discipleship,* "Earthly possessions dazzle
our eyes and delude us into thinking that they can provide security
and freedom from anxiety. Yet all the time they are the very source
of all anxiety."[1]

◊◊◊◊◊◊◊◊◊◊◊

Our speaking God goes to great lengths in Scripture to lay out
instructions designed to preserve our peace and deepen our joy. But
many of us are not experiencing this peace, wondering why the whole
thing is eluding us. We feel that we have misplaced it somehow, like
peace is wherever our keys or glasses might be. At the risk of over-
simplifying, this may be because we have, at some point, left the firm
paths God has wisely established for us for the seemingly lush and
verdant greens that our flesh and the world have long been calling us
to. As mentioned in the previous chapter, *peace* is a broad term that
encompasses more than just an internal sense of well-being, but this
inner rest is an unmatched gift we receive when we choose to live the
way God prescribes.

When we attempt to flee God's presence in order to fulfill our
lusts, racing to any port of escape, hoping to catch the last ship out

of our convicting harbor, we sacrifice this incomparable treasure. It is what happened to Jonah when he paid the fare to Tarshish in an attempt to get God off his back—forgetting to factor in that wherever he went, God was already there.

Though I like to blame my seasons of lack of peace on the disruptions around me, I am amazed at how often *I* am the undoing of my peace, independent of any outside forces. Jonah's life depicts this self-sabotage well. He was an intriguing man to whom God had given the glorious mission of carrying the message of repentance and forgiveness—an impeccably wrapped gift of grace—to the great city of Nineveh, known mostly for its evil and violence. God chose Jonah as an agent of His compassion to the people of Nineveh in a day when grace was more of a glimmer than the Bright Morning Star it is today. His mission was a profound one, a phenomenal tap on the shoulder from God, but one he refused to accept because he hated the Ninevites and couldn't bear to watch God show mercy to such a pack of unscrupulous heathens. Jonah would rather die than serve as part of their restoration. And so he ran. And this is precisely where his peace began to break up like dried leaves on the wind:

> But Jonah ran away from the LORD and headed for Tarshish. He went down to Joppa, where he found a ship bound for that port. *After paying the fare*, he went aboard and sailed for Tarshish to flee from the LORD. Then the LORD sent a great wind on the sea, and such a violent storm arose that the ship threatened to break up. (Jonah 1:3–4)

In order for us to have the money to "pay the fare," we have to sell our peace. It's the first thing to go when we lunge for the coattails of unrighteousness, not to mention the effect our choices have on the people around us. The innocent sailors were inadvertently caught up in Jonah's tempest and sent into a panic. They cried out to any god who might be awake while they cast off valuable cargo like it was meaningless weight, desperately trying to lighten the ship. Winds struck up around Jonah, and waves tossed his ship to and fro as if it were a plastic toy in the hands of God. Jonah choked his supply of peace when he chose disobedience, for God's mercy will not let us rest in our own folly: "They that observe lying vanities [cling to false gods] forsake their own mercy" (Jonah 2:8 KJV).

King David compromised his peace in similar ways, chronicling the unrest of his soul in Psalm 32:4–5:

> For day and night your hand was heavy upon me;
>   my strength was sapped as in the heat of summer.
>
> Then I acknowledged my sin to you
>   and did not cover up my iniquity.
> I said, "I will confess my transgressions to the
>   LORD"—
> and you forgave the guilt of my sin.

Sometimes we are the worst enemies of our own peace. Like David, we toss it away for sexual indulgences outside of God's perfectly tailored lines, or like Jonah, we choose our own paths to "freedom." We run to lying vanities, forsaking the mercy and peace that is ours to have.

⁓⁓⁓⁓⁓⁓

Not long ago I sat with a friend in the back room of a church just minutes before I was to speak to a group of women in Florida. I was miserably plagued with my third cold in a stretch of just a few weeks—this all-natural, no sugar, roll-your-own pasta dough is apparently getting me nowhere—exhausted from little sleep and too many middle-seat airplane rides and excessively perky flight attendants. Not to mention it was raining like all the sky had decided to take revenge on the sun, which normally shines uncontested in southern Florida. I wanted a bed and a cup of tea, not a mic and an audience—at least not in that moment.

My friend looked over at me and said the very thing that would propel me through my next two-hour-long session on the book of Ruth, "Kelly, you're tired, you're sick, it's raining, but you've got your freedom."

And with freedom comes … peace.

I knew exactly what my friend was referring to: She is close enough to me to know the seasons in my life when I have waded through the strain of relationships because of my own poor choices, when I have striven in business, not leaving room for the hand of God, and when I have plain not been obedient to Him. This has always lit up the angst meter in me. The same hand that was heavy upon David has been heavy upon me, and at times, the same type of storm that God whipped up with the snap of His fingers for Jonah,

He has seen fit to brew up in my little sea of the world. In essence, I have lived patches of my life *without* peace. Sometimes it's been fear related or circumstance induced, but often my lack of peace is a direct result of not following the loving commands of God. Being reminded of this made me realize that I wouldn't trade the peace I now have for all the Florida sunshine or rock-star immune system or first-class seats and imported nut medleys the world could offer. I would rather have a clear conscience on a rocky road than be plagued by guilt on a silver street.

That morning I took the stage weary, but I took it in peace. (Perhaps this is what is meant in Proverbs 17:1: "Better a dry crust with peace and quiet than a house full of feasting, with strife.") And when I say peace, I mean that besides the unrelenting sniffling and coughing, nothing else was nagging at me. When speaking to this expectant gathering of women, I wasn't looking over my shoulder, harboring any secret sins that were burdening me with guilt. I wasn't obsessively tormented by worry or dominated by fear. I wasn't in the middle of trying to work my way out of some tangled and sticky mess I had gotten myself into, again. Surely I will have more times when things out of my control will challenge my peace, but in so far as it lies with God and me, I have peace, and for this I am grateful.

Perhaps the relationship between a life that pursues godliness and the gift of peace is said best in Psalm 85:10: "Righteousness and peace kiss each other." They are intimately involved. You cannot have righteousness without peace or peace without righteousness. The wonderful news is that peace can be restored to our lives, even after some raucous storms brought on by our own selfish choices. And once we have it, we normally will protect it with renewed commitment and purpose. Peace will no longer be something we regard with whims of *que sera, sera*. We will guard it vigilantly by preserving our commitment to righteousness at all costs. We will have discovered that a clear conscience, and thus a restful soul, is to be prized above all worldly pleasures and relationships, because righteousness and peace stroll hand in hand.

I sat with a friend of mine in the generous lobby of a hotel in a bustling city on the East Coast recently. We brooded over politics, mused about our travels, hashed through personal discoveries and frustrations. Eventually she shared with me about a certain area in her life that had become confusing for her. She didn't know where to draw her lines. After listening to her predicament, I felt she might do better by shoring up a little closer to the heart of God. My humble opinion was strengthened by lines in my own life that at one time had been vague and blurred, ones that ended up compromising my peace. I told her that when I think of drawing moral lines in my life, I no longer shoot for the bare-minimum bounds of "okay" or "permissible," but for the much richer soil of holiness. I am not motivated out of suffocating legalism or pharisaical piousness, but by the truth that holiness protects the peace that I wildly value. And nothing is worth compromising it.

The beauty of peace is that it can be restored when we take the chisel of repentance to the stone of disobedience, and though this doesn't sound especially thrilling, it is much better if we hurry up and use our own chisel so that God doesn't have to use His—so I've found. For example, I'd much rather get my scrawny little heinie back on the shore than try my "luck" in the belly of a great fish. It is God's kindness that leads us to repentance (Rom. 2:4), the act of turning around from the sin we have served and toward the presence of God through choosing obedience. God is quick to forgive, slow to wrath, and full of compassion for those who forsake their sin and seek His forgiveness. He is eager to restore peace to our troubled hearts, because it is the way He designed us to live when we came into relationship with Him in the first place: *He Himself is our peace.*

If you are longing to find inner peace once again, if you desire God to restore to you the joy of your salvation (Ps. 51:12), may I suggest the age-old prescription of confessing your sin and turning around, while chipping disobedience from the marble. Peace will be your reward.

And Then Came the Rains

Kindness

I've become so familiar with the word *kindness* that I'm afraid I've tempered it a bit, maybe even stripped it a little of its power, at least in my own mind. Maybe this is because out of all the virtues it's the one that seems pretty doable in most settings. For instance, you may not be great at operating the backhoe of humility or the scissor lift of forgiveness, but pretty much everyone can tap the hammer of kindness, right?

When you say someone is kind, it can be as benign as saying they've got great hair or that they especially like watermelon. The compliment doesn't mean a whole lot, except that the person is really nice, which in the South ends up being pretty much everyone on your block. But when you brush up against a deep, authentic kindness in a person, you can sense that velvet or silk or something altogether special has just swept across your soul's skin, a quality that doesn't flow as freely as we might think.

One of my friends just moved to Tennessee from New York and in a perfectly serious conversation said she feels like she's relocated to a different planet. This has a little to do with the sweet tea and cheese grits, but mostly to do with the genteel manners and spirits of this region. (This is not to say that there aren't kind people in New York. It's one of my favorite places on earth. It's just that there's more honking and less waving there.) But when looking at Scripture, I realize that the virtue of kindness is a lot more potent, a lot more powerful than chipper people who smile and hug a lot, though this is all really good. In fact, I've watched the power of kindness literally save lives not long ago—a dramatic statement I'm not sure I would have bought before the greatest flood in Nashville's recorded history swept through our city (and many surrounding areas), leaving in its wake an outpouring of kindness that rivaled the torrent itself. It has made me rethink kindness altogether.

Our city had eighteen inches of rain in thirty-six hours, and I've heard it said that that amount of rainfall in that amount of time is the equivalent of a MLB player hitting 150 home runs or an NFL running back rushing for 4,000 yards in one season. Suffice it to say, this will probably not happen again in Nashville for another hundred to thousand years, maybe not ever. And the downpour came without warning, other than a weekend forecast of rain that normally makes me think of showers, not fire hydrants. No one predicted this collection of storms would hover and dump and keep unleashing on us as though the clouds were tapping the endless supply of the ocean.

The flood crept up on us subtly, and the river crested well after the rains had ceased. The rains raised creeks, seeped through foundations, and hunted down any vulnerable brick or crack it could find. Outside of the rivers, the waters weren't violent, just steady and relentless enough to pretty much destroy everything in their swell. My earthen basement had a few puddles, but other than that my house thankfully stayed dry. (My friend told me I definitely needed to get flood insurance from here on out. Considering the storm of the millennium left me with only trickles, I pondered for a second and shot back, "Actually, that's the one thing I'm pretty sure I *don't* need!")

Thousands of homes were altogether lost or partially destroyed. Some erupted in flames as water toppled over gas cans and soaked electrical wires in basements and garages. In many cases the water ravaged through ground floors, leaving the second floors remarkably untouched. The problem is, you can't walk through a war zone of buckling drywall, mold, mildew, and waterlogged furniture every day to get upstairs to your dry reading room, where you sit in your dry chair and leaf through your dry book. A second floor is obsolete without a first.

Some people lost everything, and a lot of others just lost bunches and bunches of stuff, like my friend Jason, whose stored belongings sat under eight feet of water in his basement. Our church put together a cleaning team at his house to pull out virtually every single vestige of—oh, I don't know—Christmas ornaments, leather shoes from the '80s, an electric marinater that had never been opened (I didn't know what this was, but my epicurean heart wanted it bad), window frames he was saving for his "artist" friends, and the cake topper: a Curious George cookie jar, which my friend Wendy Lee said definitely raised some questions. More than losing all this loot, I think Jason's greatest pain was the vulnerability and powerlessness of having his whole world displayed in the yard for everyone to see—there are no secrets when a flood comes roaring through. No fig leaves to hide behind. (Not that there was anything bad down in his basement, just more along the lines of pack rat-ish.)

However, for so many others, the loss was not just about incidental, superfluous stuff but about heirlooms, paintings, photo albums, beloved furniture, and the comforts and securities that are so closely tethered to having a place to call home. And now so many of those homes are flat-out gone, or no longer livable, but still attached to a monthly mortgage payment, a bill demanding payment whether or not you'll ever be able to cook dinner in the house again. That, or bankruptcy. And for all but a remnant of the flood victims, no one carried flood insurance, because when's the last time Nashville was hit with a flood of this magnitude, or a baseball player hit 150 home runs in a single season?

After the floods receded, I could have stayed in my relatively dry neighborhood, going about my daily routine, bypassing the more tactile experiences of flood cleanup, except that my church was in desperate need of a few self-employed people (people who could let their "selfs" take off) to help with the demolition process in a couple of homes. And here's the thing: The opportunity to swing a sledgehammer, rip up linoleum with a crowbar, and carry out piles of drywall with a ton of your friends is a surprisingly brilliant escape from writing. Plus I got to eat pork and pizza and not feel bad about it, because this is what the Baptists were handing out for free under their brightly colored tents. Thousands of bright faces and sturdy arms and tender hearts descended upon a ravaged subdivision in one undiluted concentration of love. If kindness were pure energy, we could have lit up New York City. People were lending one another sump pumps and generators, kids were passing out Gatorade and cold water bottles from wagons and wheelbarrows, and perfect strangers were embracing in the streets. It was one of kindness's finest moments.

Showing kindness was easy during the cleanup—at least for the first few days, because the whole thing was novel. You felt needed and part of something much bigger than yourself. The sun had come back out, and the temperatures were in the high sixties with no humidity. Adrenaline was as available as oxygen, fueled by the nobility of a community banding together in the face of daunting loss and destruction. Everyone was your friend. Together, we would not be overcome—as long as the pizza slices kept coming and the banner of camaraderie kept waving.

All of which began to fade in the second week.

The churches couldn't feed the community forever, and people had to get back to work and routines, and that thing called compassion fatigue began to set in. The block party was over. Oh, and the sharp debris that was left scattered in the streets started taking out people's tires, one of them being mine. The rains came back and the drywall powder that was coating the roads turned into a slippery sheet that almost sent me sailing in my flip-flops. (Word to the wise: Don't wear flip-flops in flood zones, if for some reason you would not have already thought of this yourself.) Everyone started to get tired. For the flood victims, the city codes and looters and debts began to deflate their hopeful spirits, while piles of red tape started wrapping around their ankles. For those who were helping, the pull of "normal" life began to tug on our abilities and energy to help. Rebuilding wouldn't be as easy as we had all thought a week ago, when spirits were high and the burgers were free. Even the face of kindness started taking a bit of a hit, as people grappled with the long road of reality that lay ahead of them. The smiles and friendly tones weren't coming as easily.

But this is where the deep and abiding virtue of kindness—the kindness that is fueled by the Holy Spirit—is set apart from the cheaper version of mere friendliness or adrenaline-based sympathy. It's when the easy-to-come-by smiles and patience and "No, you first" attitudes that can be fueled by your flesh in the early stages starts to run out, and you realize that sustainable kindness is energized by something far more enduring and powerful than the common grace of mankind—by the Person of Jesus. It's when you realize the difference between the biblical virtue of kindness and a mood, disposition, or even the culture of Southern hospitality.

ⱮⱮⱮⱮⱮⱮⱮ

My friend and I talked about this over coffee. She was staying at my house, having dropped in from out of town right in the middle of the flood's aftermath. She had witnessed firsthand the commotion as my friends and I attempted to handle our small part of the triage. Though she does not share my Christian beliefs, she told me how noble and altruistic she thought our efforts were, how we were pouring "life force" back into the planet, sharing positive energy in the form of caring for people. She chalked this up to our being more fundamentally kind by nature, less selfish or high maintenance or something. Also, it didn't hurt that we were "religious" by her estimation.

I tried to explain that God-inspired kindness is not about self-improvement or a biologically sweeter and nicer disposition. I wanted her to understand that my friends and I were not running around town helping people because we wanted to polish ourselves up through noble efforts that make us feel better about ourselves when we finally crash in our beds at night. We're not buying a whole bunch of stock in karma, hoping our kindness will one day mature into a zillion blessings of returning good fortune. And, if I can speak for my friends, kindness is not the basic disposition we were all born with. I am no less selfish or high maintenance than the next person, at least not on a fundamentally human level. I love my space and quiet and peace. Just last week I had another person staying with me who rifled through my chocolates and guzzled my farm-fresh milk straight out of its sleek, chilled bottle. This made me a little nuts. *My nonhomogenized milk!* My human nature is the same as anyone else's.

But Christ is continually transforming me, teaching me about the virtues through Scripture while giving me His Spirit to work them out in my life. What's lit up the heart of kindness in me, not just during the flood, but over the past few years, is a deep desire to reflect the love of God to the people around me because of who He is and the work He has done in my heart. Caring and kindness are not about self-betterment but the opposite, which is recognizing that my "self" is quite obviously not enough. I cannot show true, enduring kindness apart from the life of Jesus. I cannot be "better enough" to live the virtues without His life living through me. I am so aware of this that on the way to the flood zone one day, I prayed that the people whom my church was helping would see Jesus in us. It does no good if they just see me or anyone else, because I know myself too well. I cannot be anyone's ultimate savior. I long for them to see that, yes, this is the kindness of our church, but all this kindness originates from the kind heart of God. And if it's coming from anywhere else, it's just human moralism that has no enduring effect.

⌇⌇⌇⌇⌇⌇⌇⌇

Practically speaking, one of the most helpful boosts to my kindness reservoir is spending time with kind people. There are a few men and women in my life who immediately come to mind. If I can be so technical in paring back the unique things they do, along with the things they don't do, here are some of my observations: They listen. They draw others out. They express genuine interest in the lives of those who cross their paths. They're gentle. They can speak a hard truth if needed, but they deliver their words with love. They're the ones who do things like purposefully learning the waiter's name so they can say, "The mango salsa was delicious, *Jim*." They're also the ones who hang on to trifling details, like the fact that you were sniffling last weekend, and they remember to ask you if that vitamin C is doing the trick. Very plainly, I think kind people make you feel special and singled out.

Now, a word about what they don't do: Kind people don't do a lot of gossiping. I have never known a genuinely kind person whose downtime centered on unflattering stories about others or who effortlessly tore people down. Kind people aren't short-tempered or self-centered. They're not explosive. They don't talk about themselves all the time or continually hijack conversations back to their own successes or problems. They're not petty.

Of course, no one is a flawless image of kindness; these are just some of the prominent things I see and don't see in the kindest people I know.

Given some of these qualities, however, I don't think developing kindness is a process that can be merely whittled down to doing more of some things and less of others. These characteristics are the result of a transformed heart, a heart the Holy Spirit has lovingly meddled with over the years. I am much more others-oriented than I used to be—with light-years to go—and I know this is because God is giving me a greater capacity for kindness as I am eager to cooperate with Him. I desire to be encouraging and sweet to the sullen worker behind the counter or to patiently respond to the nagging relative or to take extra time with the person at the party who's needy and longs to be heard. None of this comes naturally to my personality, but kindness has become my desire. For one thing, God's been very kind to me. Specifically kind in specific instances, not just generally kind. Just taking note of these moments and seasons is a brilliant tool in developing kindness, because we can know kindness only to the degree we've been shown it by God and others.

I continue to learn kindness also through the conviction of the Holy Spirit when I am acting rashly and selfishly, when I pray that God would make me into the kind and gentle woman He desires me to be, and when I read the examples and writings in the

Bible. I think of Philippians 2:20–21, where Paul writes this about
Timothy: "I have no one else like him, who takes a genuine interest
in your welfare. For everyone looks out for his own interests, not
those of Jesus Christ." Paul's way of complimenting Timothy here
is so different from his suggesting that Timothy was looking out
for the benefits of others because it made him feel better about
himself, because he was trying to impress God, or because he was
hoping that by giving back to the universe, the universe would one
day give back to him. This form of kindness is not about Timothy
but the interests of Jesus Christ. What's so revealing about the heart
of Christ here is that the interests of others (which Timothy was
looking out for) were also *Christ's* interests. Christ is interested in
the welfare of people, and kindness is one of the greatest ways we
can show this selfless interest.

Earlier Paul says, "Each of you should look not only to your own
interests, but also to the interests of others." (Phil. 2:4). As I consider
what authentic kindness looks like, I have to be aware that one of its
most formidable enemies is selfishness, the wily foe that will bring
kindness to its knees. I have to pray against this often, because my
natural tendency is to look after my own interests and agendas. God
doesn't ask me to neglect every one of my own needs or desires or
to empty myself of every plan or pleasure I hold dear. Looking out
for the interests of others is about the posture of my heart. Does my
heart break for the people around me? Do I long to make someone
else comfortable, even if it's at the expense of my own comfort? Am I
delighted to speak a kind word of encouragement while totally frustrated with my flat tire? Is my speech generally uplifting? Do I enjoy
seeing others benefit from my sacrifices?

This is all about heart, not about doing more stuff on the outside or plastering a feigned smile. In Matthew 12:34–35, Jesus deals a scathing blow to the Pharisees' outer "righteousness" by saying, "You brood of vipers, how can you who are evil say anything good? For out of the overflow of the heart the mouth speaks. *The good man brings good things out of the good stored up in him,* and the evil man brings evil things out of the evil stored up in him." (I was tempted to include only what I've italicized and leave out the "brood of vipers" part, but I think it's good to remind ourselves that Jesus is not a tame muse or, as my pastor likes to say, our cosmic concierge. He is holy and loves justice and doesn't play lightly with those who take pride in their outer works of "righteousness" and use their good deeds for their own selfish gain.)

Since I started studying the virtues and reflecting on them while writing this book, I've realized how much the heart is central to all of them. There is simply no way to detach my heart from my actions, especially when it comes to the characteristics of Jesus. If my heart is full of pride and arrogance, I will not extend mercy and patience to the people I encounter. When my heart is tied up with jealousy and anger, kindness and forgiveness will not run freely in my life. Conversely, when God has tenderized our hearts, humbled us, and aligned us with His Spirit, we will not be able to help the overflow of kindness, joy, and love.

The excellent news of the gospel is that God has come to turn our hearts of stone into soft and docile hearts of flesh. He hasn't left us alone to figure out this kindness thing. Paul says, "But when the *kindness* and love of God our Savior appeared, he saved us, not because of righteous things we had done, but because of his mercy"

(Titus 3:4–5). God displayed His kindness to us through Jesus Christ, a kindness that He is now empowering us to live out to those around us.

᷈᷈᷈᷈᷈᷈᷈᷈᷈᷈᷈

Our words play an essential part in kindness. Jesus emphasized our speech when He said, "For out of the overflow of the heart the mouth *speaks*." My speech must genuinely reflect God's heart, whether I'm happy, tired, hot, hopeful, or cramped. In Colossians 3:12, Paul tells us to put on the clothing of kindness. He also tells us to take off "anger, rage, malice, slander, and filthy language *from [our] lips*." None of these is going to be a conduit for kindness and will instead work tirelessly against it. We can't be kind *and* slanderous, kind *and* full of cursing, kind *and* gushing with gossip, kind *and* biting with our tongues. We must season our words with the hope of the gospel and the love of Jesus with a seasoning that can only come from the Holy Spirit. In essence, a kind word is more powerful than we often imagine; it can even turn away wrath (Prov. 15:1).

Before he became a giant of the early church, Augustine of Hippo stumbled into a cathedral in Milan after leaving his home and squandering his life in wayward living. He wrote this of the pastor, Ambrose: "I began to love him, not at first, indeed, as a teacher of the truth—which I entirely despaired of in Thy Church—but as a man friendly to myself."[1] How glorious that God saw fit to lure the astonishing mind of Augustine with the simplicity of kindness. How perfectly like Him.

True kindness may be one of the most telling signs of our Christianity, the open door that the outside world first encounters. My prayer for us as the body of Christ, the living organism of His kingdom, is that before the lost souls in our midst experience our dogmas, our creeds, our values, even our theology, they will first be moved by our kindness. And how much more would they see this if we showed kindness to one another *within* the body of Christ. We need not wait another thousand years for a flood to usher it in.

Everything Must Die (To Rise Again)

Humility

After calling them in a desperate panic just moments after sunrise the other day, I saw Grassy Roots lawn service pull up to my house—probably because there was virtually nothing of my lawn that was actually grass, only greenish, weedy stalks that somewhat resembled grass.

I have no idea how spring crept up on me with so little warning, but the other day I awakened to a row of valiant daffodils swaying outside my living-room window, all brightly baring their colors against any threats of another cold snap. They banded together in the newly balmy breeze as if to say to any remaining vestiges of winter, "*Try us!*" The cherry blossoms burst forth as if on some invisible cue, and the gleeful birds formed a choir in their branches. The glory of spring was here, but so were the winter weeds and that devil Bermuda grass that threatened to slay my chances of ever having a brilliantly green lawn.

This is what sent me into a bit of a yard frenzy and prompted the call to Grassy Roots—that horrendous beige blend of grasslike species sprouting up like reckless torpedoes, conquering every square inch of what was supposed to be a lush and verdant plot of land. It was an unfair battle out there: grass against absolutely anything else that could grow out of the ground. I had awakened not only to spring but also to a chaotic battleground where the grass is threatening to secede from the union, the union being my yard.

The Grassy Roots owner was not your typical lawn guy. His hair was unusually coifed for an outdoorsy vocation, and he wore distinguished glasses. He looked more like a lecturer of Shakespeare than someone who toils in the dirt and occasionally spreads manure. His tone was friendly but serious, thorough and precise. As he assessed my lawn, he murmured things like, "Just as I suspected … you have Nashville grass." This sounded dire until I remembered that I live *in Nashville*. What else are we going for here? L.A. grass? I got the impression that Nashville grass and grass that grows in Nashville are two different things.

As he plodded through the yard, he spoke of the potential for my lawn to turn around as if he were talking about someone's troubled marriage. After a few minutes of his guiding me to various spots, pointing out unhealthy threats to my yard, and explaining what he could do to help, I almost forgot what we were talking about. I felt a growing sense of urgency to *save this marriage!* He made it clear that the responsibility would ultimately fall back on me. Though the CEO of Grassy Roots had a plan, and the resources to help me accomplish that plan, he was merely the counselor. He was intent on letting me know how much a newly seeded yard would require of me. "You will have to water every day. It might rain, but you can't count on this. You'd better be out here every day with your sprinkler—unless of course you want us to install an irrigation system, which will run you the cost of a moderately priced car."

About forty-five minutes into the conversation with my new yard therapist, I was hooked. After all, I had been diagnosed with having Nashville grass, and though I had no idea what that actually meant, it began to feel like a terminal disease that needed to be addressed with focus and determination. The difficulty with Grassy Roots's plan was that tackling one problem inevitably connected itself to another. "Well, if we're going to kill off your entire lawn, we'll probably want to bring in some topsoil and re-level. And if we're going to spend the money and time evening out the grade, I would also recommend pulling up those two ugly bushes. And if we're going to rip out the bushes, I'd want to go ahead and bulldoze that awful, chain-link fence in the back, because it's not doing a thing for your property value. But if we take out the eyesore fence, we'll definitely want to replace it with something else fairly quickly, because you run the risk of your neighbors planting or building something in its place that's *really* awful."

Pretty soon I found myself wanting to buy up the whole street. What started with an innocent hope of having someone aerate, seed, and kill off some pesky weeds was ending with an aggressive proposal to kill off everything in sight and start from scratch. It seemed the best way toward a healthy green lawn was to first destroy it completely. As my friend and songwriter Matt Maher penned in one of his songs, "Everything must die to rise again."[1] How true this feels for reasons infinitely more vital than my lawn.

〰〰〰〰〰〰〰

Though we don't know the exact dates of Jesus' death or resurrection, I appreciate that Easter is celebrated during the life-giving season of spring. We can more viscerally experience the inward, spiritual reality of life sprouting from death when we can smell the fragrant scents in the air and taste the flavor of honeysuckles floating on the warm breeze, when we can look across the street at the once-barren trees and see a million tiny green buds threatening to create something as glorious as new life itself, and when the grass is, theoretically, green again.

Though the dearth of winter is always the precursor, I'm not sure there's a straighter path to the spiritual expression of spring than humility. While all the other virtues require dying to self in some manner, humility encompasses this death most fully. In its purest form, humility isn't accomplished by pulling up a few stubborn weeds of pride here or there. The whole flesh is ripped up. It's not the loveliest of pictures, and it comes at the high price of death to self, but it is the express train to new and abundant life. When we choose to humble ourselves, we give God the opportunity get at the whole yard of our selfish and proud natures in one fell swoop, a message not lost on me when my lawn guy explained that the most effective way to a healthy green lawn was for the entire thing to first die.

And in this context, when I use words like *flesh* or *die*, or phrases like *death to self*, I mean them in biblical terms. The flesh (or self) that Paül suggests needs to be put to death in Colossians 3:5 is our earthly nature. It is that natural self that if left to its own devices will steal and kill and covet. It will have the affair and cheat on its taxes. It will gossip, brag, overeat, and curse its neighbor. And if completely out of hand it will oppress the poor, abuse the vulnerable, and even murder. Our flesh is what wars against us every time we seek to live the virtues of joy, peace, patience, kindness, forgiveness, humility, and compassion, because these expressions are contrary to what our earthly selves so ravenously crave. This is why our flesh must be pulled up at the root. Taming or trying to manage it are not effective options any more than my trying to wrangle all my purple wildflowers is going to be especially successful, apart from turning my yard into a bed of reckless weeds.

When we're at this point, the theological understanding of justification and sanctification are, once again, handy to the conversation, because in one sense our flesh (old self) has already been put to death when Jesus died on the cross. The death of the flesh is an element of justification. This being so, Paul reminds us in Romans 8:13 that we continue to put to death the misdeeds of our flesh in our everyday lives *by the Holy Spirit*—sanctification. Doing so takes the whole thing out of a legalistic slugfest approach and offers us the freedom and power of the Spirit to help us accomplish this transformation. And when it comes to the virtue of humility, we will most certainly need Him. Especially when we read things such as Philippians 2:5–8:

> Your attitude should be the same as that of Christ
> Jesus:
>
> Who, being in very nature God,
> did not consider equality with God something to
>   be grasped,
> but made himself nothing,
> taking the very nature of a servant,
> being made in human likeness.
> And being found in appearance as a man,
> he humbled himself
> and became obedient to death—
>   even death on a cross!

The course that Jesus took is wildly different from the natural bents of our minds and our culture, which are set on advancing and exalting the self. The mind and attitude of Christ propelled Him to take on the very form and nature of a servant, and though equality with God was rightfully His, He did not consider it something to be clutched at the expense of rescuing us. He took on the lowly and limited form of man. He laid down incomprehensible pleasures and privileges for the prize of redeeming humankind. And though He never forfeited His divinity, He emptied Himself of all His glories and rights. He became obedient, a non-negotiable element of humility, to death, even the lowly and despised death on a cross.

These are difficult words for me to write because of that opening line in Philippians: "Your attitude should be *the same* as that of Christ Jesus." Or in the King James wording I grew up with: "Let this mind be in you...." If only we could just stand in awed admiration of the amazing and wondrous sacrifice of Jesus, thank Him, and get on with our self-promotion and vigorous protection of our "rights" and the pursuit of the pleasures we so lust after. But it's that opening line that hooks us, that lets us know that Jesus' humble disposition is not an attribute to merely appreciate but to take on as our own.

Oswald Sanders said it this way: "He deliberately chose the lowliest place that He might evidence the attitude of mind He expected in His disciples."[2] And this is precisely why something in me recoils as I write about the mind of Jesus. It's not something merely to applaud but something to actually live. Living humility is hard because it's death to self. (And also the path to abundant life—an upside-down approach to be certain, but wonderfully true. Humility's end result is spring for the spirit.)

It's important to note that it is Christ's attitude that is to be in us, not necessarily an exact mimicking of His actions. Most of us won't physically die as a result of obedience. And it is not in our realm of options to humble ourselves by leaving our place in heaven with God. But the attitude that drove Jesus to leave what was rightfully His, become a servant, and operate within self-imposed limits so that His love for us would know no limits is the same attitude we are to have.

Paul shows how this attitude works itself out tangibly: "Do nothing out of selfish ambition or vain conceit, but in humility consider others better than yourselves. Each of you should look not only to your own interests, but also to the interests of others" (Phil. 2:3–4). Paul understood how difficult it is for us to relinquish what is rightfully ours for the sake of others and to humble ourselves before loved ones, strangers, acquaintances, even enemies in our lives while treating them with esteem. He calls us to abandon our selfish ambitions. He pleads with us to stop making choices inspired by vanity and arrogance.

And if you don't feel downright pompous at the moment, it doesn't mean you get to wiggle off the hook. We often stroke our flesh and conceit in much subtler ways that are cloaked in our most seemingly pious actions. Sanders wrote, "Even in religious circles there is often an unseemly jockeying for position which is entirely alien to the mind of Christ, who stripped Himself of all privilege, renounced all pomp and power, and allowed His creatures to sneer, 'Is not this the carpenter's son?' Do we have the mind of Christ in this?"[3]

〰〰〰〰〰〰

A few months ago I was speaking at a humble church off the beaten path. Though typically I covet local coffee shops over large chains, this was one of those times when a Starbucks tea would have done the trick nicely. However, the closest Starbucks was a day's journey away.

When I walked inside the church building, I will admit to inwardly eschewing the dated aesthetics, and though I try not to let crowd size add or take away from any measure of self-worth or success I perceive I have, I was a little discouraged that the women present were peppered across the pews in a way you could precisely number with a glance. Perhaps I was tired, or perhaps I had gotten too big for my britches (though I'm not sure I understand this colloquialism—if

I ever get too big for my pants, I assume I will be feeling fat and awful, not really awesome). But at any rate, I had maybe become a little prideful, thinking I was beyond what I perceived to be an unsophisticated small group of women. And if I didn't think I had surpassed them, because logically I know this isn't true, I definitely wasn't excited about them. I was fighting for the mind of Christ, but it felt about as close as the Starbucks.

While speaking from the stage, I was wrestling my bruised flesh, trying to conjure up some spiritual pleasure in getting to talk about false gods to a small "non-prestigious" group. Though a topic of vital importance to me, the whole thing was feeling stale. I wasn't enjoying being up there, and I'm perfectly awful at acting, so it was a real challenge to push through. I wear my emotions on my entire body, which can be madly frustrating, because even when I do my Oscar-winning best to mask my melancholy mood, I will inevitably get from one of my friends, "So what's wrong with *you?*"

Despite this fact, I was hoping the women weren't sensing my inner turmoil. (It was one of those moments on stage when you pray there are no prophetesses in the crowd.) While continuing to speak as faithfully as I knew how and desperately trying to breathe life into my anemic motions, I had an encounter with God. I had just emerged onto the stage from one of the backroom offices where I had prayed and read Scripture not thirty minutes before, so I wasn't sure why God was choosing to speak right *now*. Why He didn't take that perfect opportunity when we were by ourselves and a group of unsuspecting women weren't intently gazing in my direction. The Holy Spirit said something along the lines of, "You're not enjoying this because no one in this crowd can do anything for you."

When God speaks in His indescribable yet unmistakable voice, He has a way of cutting through our endless layers of emotions and justifications and reasonings, striking the heart dead center.

Suddenly all my restlessness made sense: I was unhappy because my speaking had become self-serving—I wanted to do it only if it did something for me. And this wasn't the place where a lot could be done for me. No big churches down the street with plushier accommodations that might hear of me. No powerful, connected people in the crowd. There were no accolades from these women that I would have particularly valued, very much to my own loss. I know, I know, I sound like your worst stereotypical sketch of a "professional" Christian that ever was, which is why this part of being a writer—at least if I'm going to be authentic—is unfortunate, because sometimes I have to commit the cruddiness of my heart to something as lasting and irreversible as print. But this is just the honest truth. Teaching that day wasn't especially thrilling, because the women didn't have anything especially thrilling to offer me. And I could never have figured this out on my own. It took the Holy Spirit to reveal it to me. Again, we must depend on God to put our flesh to death.

Thankfully, in this instance, the remedy of a tendered heart came fairly quickly for me. As soon as I could get off of the stage I bee-lined it to that same quiet room I had sat in before, bowed my head, heart, and soul, and agreed with God about what He had revealed to me. It was a lot to process, but I knew it was truth in the deepest places, and I could feel it cleansing me, like Murphy's Oil being taken to the hard-to-reach crevices of my ungrateful, frustrated, haughty heart. I was thankful He had exposed the selfishness there, even if it was unflattering and happened to be in the middle of my teaching. (I probably didn't make a lick of sense after that revelation and returning to the stage. I'm sure the women were thinking, *What's with the city girl?*). I told God how much I wanted to delight in these exact women and that I didn't need a thing from them. I was there to serve, not to be served (Matt. 20:28), a concept that I had somehow misplaced during my travels.

I think it's easy to lose this charge of serving regardless of what line of work you're in. A person is not somehow safeguarded from selfish ambition and pride just because he or she is in ministry. I don't know what it's like in other parts of the world, but our Western Christian industry is in many ways set up no differently from secular ones. We have magazines that rank the fastest-growing churches and list the most highly influential Christian voices in our country. We have award shows and charts and best-seller lists. We measure ourselves by size and funding and notoriety. We push product and promote, we market and we write reviews for what's been marketed. We blog and tweet our achievements to as many people as we can coax to follow our profoundly "important" lives. And collectively we make a lot of money. (Note, I said *collectively*; I'm still trying to figure out how to pay for grass.) I am not weighing in on whether I think any of this is inherently good or evil; I'm just saying it's so. And the fact that it is so makes my job no less immune to the pull and peril of pride than anyone else's.

"Let this mind be in you." Recapturing an attitude of humility in my heart was the work of God that day. It also needed my cooperation, my willingness to agree with Him about my pride and desire for a more notable platform. My mind had to change. I had to choose the hidden reward of selflessly ministering to women who seemed different from me, who didn't have a lot to offer in the ways I valued. I needed to recognize that serving them was a privilege. I needed to be reminded that climbing the "famous ladder" and being in front of powerful and positioned people have nothing to do with why God opened up doors for me to travel and communicate Scripture in the first place. In fact, I would say these things are precisely what my calling is *not* about. When I'm walking closely to the heart of God, this is a relieving truth. Any one of us may have public successes and fame, great reviews and promotions—all of which can be blessings—but when they are the catalysts for what we do, our minds are alien to that of Christ's. We find that vain conceit and not humility is leading us.

〰〰〰〰〰

Death to the self is never an *Oooh, pick me! Pick me!* kind of activity. Humbling ourselves before others and before God comes at the price of our ravenous flesh that is always crying out for esteem and pleasure. But we receive a much truer honor and durable joy when we choose humility, because God Himself rewards it in a way that is much more satisfying than filling up on the cotton candy our basic natures crave.

After describing Jesus' descent to earth, Paul expresses this promise:

> Therefore God exalted him to the highest place
>   and gave him the name that is above every name,
> that at the name of Jesus every knee should bow,
>   in heaven and on earth and under the earth,
> and every tongue confess that Jesus Christ is Lord,
>   to the glory of God the Father. (Phil. 2:9–11)

Death of our pride and selfish ambition is endured only so something much more glorious can be resurrected in its place. On the night before Jesus was betrayed, when all the disciples were arguing about who was the greatest, Jesus explained that earthly kings lord their authority over their people, fighting for promotion and honor at any cost. *"But you are not to be like that,"* He said. "Instead, the greatest among you should be like the youngest, and the one who rules like the one who serves" (Luke 22:26). Their entire way of thinking needed to be reworked, as does mine on a regular basis. It's like I need humility maintenance, a "Let this mind be in you" tune-up after daily submergences in a world that lives off the promotion and preservation of self.

If the idea of humility or the process of getting there is still fuzzy, my encouragement is simple: Take note of where your pride is being chipped at, whether by a person or circumstance, and bring it before God as an offering. Don't fight the process. If a spouse or friend has spoken painful truths to you, let humility do its work by listening without defense or anger. When you find your pride flaring up over and over, when you notice your circle of friends is shrinking because you have disregarded people who aren't of your class or status, if you're constantly in defense mode with everyone around you, the virtue of humility may be the medicinal balm your heart needs. Ask God to reveal your pride, the self that won't budge and tirelessly needs to be fed, so you can bow into the freeing posture of humility before God and others.

∿∿∿∿∿∿∿

The same night Jesus adjusted the thinking of His disciples in the upper room, He went on to explain their ultimate destiny: "so that you may eat and drink at my table in my kingdom and sit on thrones, judging the twelve tribes of Israel" (Luke 22:30). Just as God exalted Jesus to the highest place after He had humbled Himself, so Jesus promised to exalt the disciples after lives of servanthood. Spring is always on its way for the heart willing to bow in humility. Life in its deepest colors and fullest blooms is percolating beneath the cold, fallow ground of dying to our pride. True greatness, as valued by our Creator, is found in such a death. "For everything must die to rise again."

When the Crowds Keep Marching

Compassion

I have decided that after plodding through the miry swamp of dying to self, the other side is an existence more invigorating than any other. You may not think of the tight path of humility and the word *invigorating* as going together like imported cheese and olives, but they are a surprisingly complementary pair. Jesus beautifully explained in John's gospel that unless a kernel of wheat falls to the ground and dies, it remains a single seed. But if it dies, it produces many seeds from which the nourishing wheat springs. Whoever loses his life will gain it.

When we live out of pride, we are left to tirelessly protect the single seed of life, but when we live with the posture of humility and die to ourselves, we allow God to turn our one life into an abundant harvest that reaches so far beyond ourselves we will scarcely believe what God can do with a single life that chooses to die in the soil of His hands.

I have discovered that when I live out of a spirit of humility, I become connected with people I may never have noticed or might have passed by in my blind arrogance. Humility is not too good for anyone's race, color, or sullied past. It cannot look down upon, because it constantly reminds us that "There but for the grace of God go I." Because humility is not encumbered by the need to look up to the false gods of prestige, power, or position, it sees clearly. And this is invigorating because suddenly the entire world is opened up to us, and we discover that the common road of suffering has brought us into relationship with people who never before had entrance into our cool, isolated circles. Not that any of us blatantly think we have cool, isolated circles, but we do. And living with humility busts these wide open.

$$\sim\!\!\sim\!\!\sim\!\!\sim\!\!\sim\!\!\sim$$

I was sitting with an acquaintance at a dinner party a few months back. The acquaintance also happens to be a counselor, which I tend to find a threatening combination. This person is as warm and inviting as she can be, but when you know someone's a counselor, you can't help wondering the whole night if the way you held your glass or asked for the salt might be tipping her off as to whether or not you need to be on medication. (Clearly this may be my own problem.)

At any rate, she asked me why I had such a heart for women who had gotten out of prison, especially for the ones bound by the fetters of drugs, alcohol abuse, and prostitution. I had to weigh my response thoughtfully, because I've never felt a specific call on my life for these women in particular. I don't have any deep connection with addiction or incarceration. So as I fumbled for an eloquent response, I realized that for me it doesn't matter if it's the prisoner, the drug abuser, the wealthy businesswoman who fights depression, or the upstanding Christian who's just dying because she still doesn't have a husband or a child—brokenness draws me.

I may feel this way because the Lord has carried me through significant seasons of humbling and brokenness in my own life, narrow tunnels that hid some of life's most precious gifts, treasures from breaking experiences that I will never release from up against my chest. When you know suffering and humbling, you become intimate with humility, and when humility becomes your friend, it opens you up to a world you never knew before. A world in desperate need of compassion from those who see, care, and are willing to tangibly offer it. A spirit of humility effortlessly displays this kind of God-given compassion, whereas it's impossible for an arrogant, self-absorbed soul to readily bend this way to the lowly. I have found humility to be the precursor to true compassion.

◦◦◦◦◦◦◦◦◦◦◦◦

A few mornings ago I read about the blind beggar in Luke 18:35–43. The sun was blazing through the windows after a particularly long and dismal winter. My soul was aching for the same kind of penetrating warmth from the voice of God. I was prepared to skim through the end of the chapter, because I had heard about Blind

Bartimaeus since I was a small child perched in my Sunday school chair in my dress and patent leathers. I even sang songs about him in junior high youth group: "Blind man stood by the road and he cried," *clap, clap*. (I can't begin to tell you why after such a sobering lyric we clapped.)

But of course, as soon as I think I have something relatively down, like the story of the blind man begging by the roadside, God uncovers something I haven't yet seen. That morning I was given one of those glimmering nuggets worthy of relishing.

"Those who led the way" rebuked him and told him to be quiet, but he shouted all the more, 'Son of David, have mercy on me!'" Luke's is the only gospel that specifies the condemning voices came from the leaders of the crowd. They viewed the ailing man, with no sight and no coins in his pockets, as an embarrassing nuisance worthy only of their dismissal. After all, he was getting in the way of their mission *with* Jesus. They tried to snuff out his desperate cries—not just selfishly passing him but declaring that his request for mercy was not worthy to be uttered, much less granted.

Those who led the way. It is a frightening revelation. To think that the leaders of this crowd, barreling toward Jericho like storm clouds rolling across the sky, felt justified in condemning the vulnerable and needy, with Jesus right in their midst. It is a startling picture of the often-misleading power of a group mentality, a deceptive influence that can work its way even through a religious crowd. How easy it is to get swept up in its rhythm, marching to the beat of religious mission, convinced we are keeping in step with Jesus—even leading the way—when suddenly we realize that at some point, maybe even way back, Jesus has stopped. And there we stand miles ahead, beating on some hollow drum, realizing we have missed the very heart of the gospel: showing the compassion of Jesus to the least of these.

"Jesus stopped and ordered the man to be brought to him. When he came near, Jesus asked him, 'What do you want me to do for you?'" I think compassion is always coupled with action. True compassion anyhow. It's easy to offer sympathy with a quick prayer or deep sigh but another thing altogether to stop our forward movement in the midst of the pressing crowd of our schedules and agendas and "Jesus work," and offer to *do* something. In the gospels we find Jesus demonstrating and teaching, over and over, that action is an integral part of compassion. It is not a bonus or shiny cherry on top but part of its very nature:

> When Jesus landed and saw a large crowd, he had com-passion on them *and healed their sick.* (Matt. 14:14)

> Jesus called his disciples to him and said, "I have compassion for these people; they have already been with me three days and have nothing to eat. I do not want to send them away hungry, or they may collapse on the way." … *Then he took the seven loaves and the fish, and when he had given thanks, he broke them and gave them to the disciples, and they in turn to the people.* (Matt. 15:32, 36)

> Jesus had compassion on them and touched their eyes. Immediately they received their sight and fol-lowed him. (Matt. 20:34)

Filled with compassion, Jesus reached out his hand *and touched the man.* "I am willing," he said. "Be clean!" (Mark 1:41)

When Jesus landed and saw a large crowd, he had compassion on them, because they were like sheep without a shepherd. So he began teaching them many things. (Mark 6:34)

[Jesus said,] "So he got up and went to his father. But while he was still a long way off, his father saw him and was filled with compassion for him; *he ran to his son, threw his arms around him and kissed him.*" (Luke 15:20)

wwwwwww

A few days after being moved by the story of Bartimaeus, I was challenged with this message to stop and *do.* (God rarely enlightens us for our mere theological knowledge so we can kick up our feet and toast our C. S. Lewis selves.)

I had a presentation for the staff of the recovery program I work with regarding a curriculum I was helping to put together. I was on a tight schedule, mostly because of this book, which has managed to coil its tendrils around my every waking moment of consciousness. (Oh, the romance of writing.)

On my way up the lethargic elevator—the kind you're pretty sure you could have beaten if you took the stairs carrying a small elephant—I ran into one of the girls from my weekly Bible study. She had just found out that her weekend pass from the program was being revoked because her case manager didn't think the boy she had just met, and who wanted her to spend the night with him, would be a healthy way to fritter away her Saturday night. For someone who has never hung around long enough to experience the ramifications of the word *no,* my friend was preparing to walk out the doors of the program for good.

I so did not have time to stay and talk her out of it. The crowd of looming deadlines, and bills, and post-office runs, and a car so coated in pollen that pretty much everyone I drove by had to dab their eyes in its wake was chanting, "Be quiet. I don't have time for your boy and authority problems! I have to get to the car wash and write a chapter on *compassion.*" In the midst of the cacophonous crowd, I heard Jesus asking me to stop. But stopping was not part of my agenda. My urgent, ever-important list was staring me down with not a single line sliced through any of its tasks.

But I knew I had heard God's voice. And at this point in my relationship with Him, I find it much easier to go ahead and heed Him on the spot than be all churned up for the rest of the day, fighting and squirming, futilely trying to justify why I didn't do what He'd asked me to do in the first place. It's just plain not worth it to me anymore. And so my friend and I settled into the quaint library of her group home, and I tabled that blustery crowd in my mind. And I stopped. And she lamented. And I listened. And then I comforted her with the comfort I have received from Christ at various times in my life. ("Praise be to the God and Father of our Lord Jesus Christ, the Father of *compassion* and the God of all comfort, who comforts us in all our troubles, *so that we can comfort those in any trouble with the comfort we ourselves have received from God*"—2 Cor. 1:3–4.)

This isn't always the case in these scenarios, but it was the best hour of my day. I encountered another soul in its deepest places and offered the comfort and wisdom I had gleaned from submitting myself to authority, even if I had bucked and thrashed in the process like a fuming fish on its hook. My friend's countenance lightened, and I think she may have even grasped that conundrum of someone loving us enough to tell us no. We prayed, and I gave her one of those hugs that wasn't just obligatory but an embrace I could actually feel. I could tell the compassion I had for her was being drawn up from a bubblier well, no longer measured in duty but in love.

I left her contemplating in the deep, cozy chair she had relaxed in during our talk, and I told her that if she left the program because she couldn't go see her "boyfriend," I'd have to do something really drastic. This posed no threat whatsoever, because intimidating I am not, but it felt good to wield an imaginary warning. She later told me she had fallen asleep after I left her, perhaps in deep consideration of all my exquisite wisdom, or out of unrelenting boredom from listening to me yammer about the blessings of authority. Either way, it surprised her that she'd drifted off in the middle of the day, awkwardly exposed in the corner of the library. Inside I smiled, thinking how tenderly the blanket of compassion had wrapped her up, taking her angered and restless spirit and putting it to rest.

My Jeep didn't get washed that day, but as I drove away in a puff of golden soot, all I could think was, *Who cares?* And the best part:

When I showed up on Wednesday for Bible study, my friend was still there.

⁓⁓⁓⁓⁓⁓⁓

When Jesus asked the blind beggar, "What do you want me to do for you?" it was a question that embodied two important qualities. First, it indicated that Jesus was willing to offer more than lip service by actually doing something. But, second, it took into account the desires of Bartimaeus's heart. Jesus didn't tell him what he needed but asked him what he wanted. Jesus started His encounter with what was important to Bartimaeus, at the place of his felt need. I see this as crucial to compassion, as we must let people know we care about what's important to them, not just what's important to us for them.

Like my friend's case manager, I too thought that her spending the night with a man she's known a whopping ten days was a wildly disastrous idea, but it wouldn't have been wise for me to start there—at least not in this situation. I first had to understand her longings, listen to her desires, and then hopefully offer another solution to her loneliness. Maybe not one as immediately gratifying but more satisfying in the long run. I don't think it's all that helpful to first greet the poor, or the vulnerable, or the depressed, or the weak with our assessments of what they need, along with our impressive resumes of how we can swoop in to save the day. We must honor them by listening first, even if their wants are beyond our reach or what is good for their well-being.

When I asked my friend what she wanted for her weekend, she said, "I want to get out of here!" That I could handle. There were lots of ways for her to get out of her dorm without depositing herself in an almost-stranger's bed. When I offered her church with me as a viable option, she looked at me blankly, but hey, at least she knew someone cared. Someone had asked her what *she* wanted. And when we ask, "What do you want?" we let the person know we care about what's important to them.

"Lord, I want to see." (I love that Bartimaeus referred to Jesus as the "Son of David" and "Lord," two titles that showed his great esteem for the Messiah. It's interesting that the man who couldn't see somehow saw more than the crowd's pious leaders.) Bartimaeus wanted to absorb the colors of a sunset, watch the mesmerizing effects of the wind, follow the path of a butterfly. In Matthew's account of the same story, he says that in response to Bartimaeus's request, Jesus had *compassion* on him. And this compassion moved Jesus to restore his sight. Blind Bartimaeus was no longer blind—a much more appropriate spot for the *clap, clap*.

It is true that Jesus has supernatural powers that reach beyond our garden-variety assortment of impressive acts. But we cannot excuse ourselves from compassion simply because we don't have it up our sleeves to halt cancer cells or heal optic nerves (though God may occasionally grant this through us). There is plenty we *can* do. And the opportunities are all around us. If we don't feel tugged by these opportunities or are too hurried to stop for anyone but ourselves or our immediate community, then it may be an issue of compassion or lack thereof. As with all the virtues, compassion has many enemies, but selfishness is at the top of the list. Next in line is probably a fear of what we might have to encounter in the face of suffering and loss.

God has grown me in compassion and continually stretches my capacity with each new meeting with those who hurt and struggle. I have so much self-centeredness that blocks the way and so many fears that are rooted in my longing for comfort and familiarity. I don't naturally love sacrifice. But I find that my capacity for compassion is like a balloon that expands when the air of Christ's comfort is breathed into my own afflictions. When I go to Jesus in my sufferings, He comforts me with a comfort that I can then blanket upon others who are similarly hurting (2 Cor. 1:3–7).

So when we find ourselves numb to the needs of others, it may be because we have not recently, or ever, let Jesus tend to us in the place of our own woundedness. We have no supernatural comfort to extend to others because we ourselves have not been comforted. How fitting that when Christ comforts me in a certain area, I become eager to wrap up another sufferer in such comfort, while the fear of the unknown and the sacrifices of time or money grow mysteriously pale. We cannot give what we have not received. And what we receive from God we cannot help but extend to others.

∿∿∿∿∿∿∿

In two months I will return to the Amazon to ride down that vast river so I can visit some of the most remarkable people in the world. And to consume a lot of beans, of course. It's like a cruise in that there's a boat that floats on water, but the resemblance ends there. I'll sleep (in theory) in a hammock on the boat, and during the day I'll help put on camps, pass out balls and Bibles, and serve pasta to gaping little mouths like baby birdies panting for worms. I'll take this trip with dear friends and family, and if it's anything like my previous visit, I know it will forever change me.

After our trip to Brazil last year, several of us touched down in the States surprised to find ourselves suddenly stymied here in our cushy environments, doggy paddling in our deep resources. As we discussed our wealth (relatively speaking) with one another, the *real* work seemed to be outside of our own communities. But one of my closest friends appropriately reeled us back to center with her timely wisdom: "We can travel thirty-one hundred miles to Brazil or we can walk thirty-one feet to our neighbor." *Touché*.

The truth is both journeys need to be taken. It's just that we often miss what's right in front of us for the seemingly greater need across the ocean. It's like the crowd that had "bigger" work to do with Jesus in Jericho, practically tripping over the guy who lay in the middle of their path. Compassion is not just for the missionary or slum worker *over there*. It's not a virtue singled out exclusively for the pastor or AIDS worker. In Colossians 3:12, compassion is the virtue Paul tells every believer to clothe himself in, and he lists it first. When people meet us, if compassion is not the first thing they encounter, how many more shots will we get? One of my dear singer friends likes to greet me after long absences by stretching herself out as if she has wings, exclaiming, "Get into my arms!" I think compassion does this. (In a less invasive way perhaps, if you're not a hugger.)

I think out of all the virtues, the church has lost its way with this one the most. We are so big on telling everyone what they need to do and how to live up to our standards, overlooking the fact that this doesn't exactly light up the compassion meter. We haven't listened first. We haven't waited to hear and understand the needs and longings of the people around us. The church rarely asks the world what they want, as Jesus asked Bartimaeus what he wanted. If we did, they just might tell us, and then we might be responsible to engage them on a meaningful level—perhaps by tending to the desires of their hearts. This is not a weak, watered-down expression of our faith, giving people whatever they crave or encouraging them to live by whatever standards blow their way, but a love that ultimately points people toward our Savior.

"Jesus said to him, 'Receive your sight; your faith has healed you.'"

This is a two-part statement: Jesus generously gave him what he wanted while providing him with what he desperately needed: forgiveness of sins, salvation, relationship with Christ, and spiritual wholeness. Sometimes people are so thirsty or hungry or financially stuck they can't even begin to think about what they need spiritually for what they lack physically.

Bartimaeus saw the trees and the sky and his former mockers, but then *he praised God.* Compassion's arrow is always aimed at the grace and mercy of Jesus. He is compassion's final destination. This is what sets Christian compassion apart from secular social justice. Our compassion is pointing the way to Someone. Social justice is an end in itself, to help people and make their lives better. But God-inspired compassion doesn't stop at the bettering of a physical life. It extends beyond the restoring of sight, filling of bellies, granting of education, and heralds the way to Jesus. So that the people we shower with compassion will, like Bartimaeus, follow and praise God.

Of course our compassion does not discriminate against those who may not be ultimately interested in following Jesus. In Luke 17

Jesus healed ten lepers, but only one returned to thank Him. Only one was interested in truly knowing Him, yet He showed compassion to them all, cleansing every last ravaged spot whether they wanted Him or just His blessings. Expressing compassion is not a deal we strike with people only if they are willing to adhere to our set of beliefs or join our church or even worship our God. How many people would Christ have turned away if He had only extended compassion to those who returned His love?

I wonder how differently our culture would experience the church if we put on the virtue of compassion, maybe even first, as Paul lists it in Colossians. What if the people we live with or work with didn't first slam up against our steely shields of pride or judgment but fell into the graceful arms of saved sinners? Sure, we may still have to tell someone not to sleep with her boyfriend, or inform people that authority is not the vile word our culture has made it out to be. We will have to speak truth, and we will not be able to bend on the law of God that has been given for our freedom. Compassion is not amoral. But it is loving. It is eager to *do* something. It is available to stop. Most of all, it is willing to let the "holy" crowd keep marching.

More Than a Disposition
Patience

If patience is a run of hearts, I think most of us come into this world with a handful of clubs and spades. There are a few exceptions out there, people who have wonderfully mild dispositions with inconceivably long fuses. They are the ones who if stuck in a line are content to gaze at the playful squirrels outside the window or strike up a friendly conversation with whoever happens to be behind or in front of them, all with utter cheeriness. Life is not a dead sprint for them—they are not blasting toward the finish line on the brink of an aneurism while balancing their espressos. They tend to find contentment wherever they are, thus always having a certain measure of patience on hand.

My aunt Carol on my mom's side is one of these patient exceptions (important distinction, because no Minters are anything like this). Her easygoing temperament was almost canonized last Christmas during an enormous snowfall that trapped her on the highway during a trip from Georgia to Virginia to visit my family. She and my cousin inadvertently had gotten caught in one of the largest snowstorms in recent history—again, something that would have never happened to a Minter, not with newfangled inventions like the television and weathermen. (It's not like a loose hatch in the sky accidentally popped open and out came twenty-four inches of snow smothering the East Coast. We all *knew* the storm was coming before it happened.)

Nonetheless, my aunt and cousin were stuck in all this slippery mess, turning a doable twelve-hour drive into a debilitating crawl that took something closer to thirty. The fascinating piece in all this is that my aunt was unfazed by the endless piles of cars barricading her from Christmas festivities, not at all ruffled by the motionless wait. I remember her telling me, between hysterical chortles, how "cute" the snowplows were, how "interesting" she found watching them to be. And instead of frittering away her waiting in lament, she viewed the unrelenting hours in the car with no possible place to go as a gift of time to be cherished with her daughter. *Cherished.*

Now that's just plain personality. It has to be. I'm not saying that the work of the Holy Spirit can't accomplish this; I'm just saying that some people's dispositions are more naturally relaxed. More intrinsically patient. And then there are the rest of us.…

But here's the hopeful piece for the high-strung and intense: The patience Paul is talking about in Colossians 3:12 is the Greek word *makrothumia,* and it means "the quality of a person who is able to avenge himself, yet refrains from doing so. *It is patience in respect to persons,* while *hupomone,* endurance, is putting up with things or circumstances."[1] When the biblical writers speak of having patience (*makrothumia*), they are describing a patience that is people oriented, a virtue far beyond an equable temperament. At first this may sound like bad news, a double impossibility for the rest of us mere mortals. But this type of patience is something the Holy Spirit works out in our lives, not a quality we're "lucky" enough to be born with.

It's also distinct in that it's not about the endurance needed in hardships or trying circumstances (although these are great spiritual qualities to have), but is rather about forbearing with the hurts and burdens and weaknesses of the people around us. So even if you're not super relaxed by nature, or if you don't get a huge kick out of snowplows while chained to the interstate, you can still develop the deep and abiding virtue of people patience that God is able to work out in us all.

⁓⁓⁓⁓⁓⁓⁓

As with all the other virtues, I find it essential to first consider the ways God has demonstrated His patience toward me. And I will be the first to tell you that when my patience is wafer-thin, and people offer up things like, "Well, just think of how patient God has been with *you,*" I usually find it as effective as, "Eat your glazed carrots, because think of all the people who don't have vegetables to eat." And yet the sentiment is true. When I take the time to honestly reflect over the breadth of my life, I become more deeply aware of how patient the heart of God has been with me.

It has taken this passage of time for me to more fully appreciate God's patience with me, mostly because patience exists best over
time—there is no such thing as patience that lasts only a couple of
minutes. So given this time, I'm now able to look back and see the
tender and steady hand of God that has gathered me from deep in
the woods, gently setting my feet back on the narrow path many
times over. And when I didn't want to be rescued from my will-
ful excursions, I see that He waited for me with longsuffering, not
vengefully counting the time against me yet eager for my return.
(Not to say that patience is void of consequences or even discipline,
as these will be part of God's active patience with us at times. See
Hebrews 12:4–13.)

God's relentless patience has met me much like ocean waves
rolling onto the shore—there's always another round if I don't get it
the first time, or the hundred-and-thirty-second. He does not cease
showing me the same lessons over and over until the light finally
blinks on in my dull understanding and I really *get it*. His longsuffering has borne with me over the many pale idols I have so zealously
looked to for life. Whether it was running after the false gods of a
shimmering music career, the fading glow of earthly "success," or the
hope that a human could fill me up from the bottom of my heart
to the tip of my soul, God expended many patient years revealing to
me the futile pursuit of happiness apart from His presence being the
very core of all I desire. I was like a little Tarzan swinging from one
newfound god to the next, tasting the fruit of each tree, when all the
while the Lord kept saying, "Kelly, you don't want the tree; you want
the Author of the forest!" Oh, how indebted I am to the persistent,
unwavering patience of God.

When I deeply consider this divine patience, I am required to contend with how patient I am with others. I simply cannot have a good handle on the long forbearance in which God has dealt with me and consistently blow up at my neighbor. It is incongruent for me to joy in His patience while having those nagging thoughts about the people around me, the ones that go something like, *Come on, get it together already!* But when I'm authentically grateful for the ways God has shown me such enduring patience. I can feel my spirit softening, like a meat tenderizer being taken to my heart (for those of you omnivores who have ever beaten chicken breasts before).

‚ÄövvvvvvvvvvvvvÀ

This tenderness resonates with what speaker and author Beth Moore writes in her Bible study *Living Beyond Yourself* about the virtue of patience: "Everywhere you discover the word *makrothumia,* you find some form of mercy."[2] What a gleaming insight to recognize that the beating pulse of mercy is what pushes life through the veins of patience. Anyone who has ever had to forbear with another recognizes the tenderness of mercy to be a priceless companion to patience, an essential helpmate to its staying power.

I see this truth of mercy fueling patience threaded throughout Jesus' actions in the gospels. I'm not sure He ever spoke the specific word *patience,* but He embodied it at every turn. With large crowds tugging at His garments, seeking food and healing, He was never too bothered. Even when desperate people found Him in deserted places, He never snapped or scolded. Not in the midst of the pressing masses, nor in the face of the disciples' slow understanding. And when the little children longed to come to Him (and His followers impatiently dismissed them), Jesus warmly welcomed their bustling energy. He didn't turn people away, constantly present with their questions and hungers and sicknesses. Once, in His full humanity, He did wonder how long He would have to strive with the present, unbelieving generation, but He persevered all the way to His death. And He did it without flaw.

His patience was not just for the needy, burdensome, and slow-witted but also for sinners and the people who hated Him. If part of patience is refraining from taking the revenge one could take, then Jesus demonstrated patience in extraordinary measures. In the face of religious leaders who hated Him, who criticized Him, spit in His face, condemned Him to death, even mocked Him on the cross, He embodied patience by choosing to remain silent, refraining from striking back, even praying for His crucifiers, saying, "Father, forgive them, for they do not know what they are doing" (Luke 23:34). Yes, Jesus showed mercy, forgiveness, and self-control in these moments, but it was patience that held them all together as our longsuffering God put vengeance on hold.

Such divine longsuffering stands out against our slim reserves and brittle nerves. When thousands of hungry followers needed dinner, Jesus could have adopted the disciples' human logic: "It's late, we're tired—send them back to the village where they can buy their *own* grilled cheese!" But Jesus said, "I have compassion for these people; they have already been with me three days and have nothing to eat. I do not want to send them away hungry, or they may collapse on the way" (Matt. 15:32). Again, Jesus' mercy is the fuel that kept the flame of His patience burning. His patience didn't wane after days of miraculous healings, and He asked His disciples yet again, "How many loaves do you have?" (Matt. 15:34). These words weren't spoken after a restful sabbatical but after three days of tirelessly healing the mute, the lame, and the blind. To choose to keep a swarming mass of need and hunger with Him, after all He had done, went well beyond what common grace would have suggested. But I think that's what makes patience *patience*. It keeps mercy and compassion flowing when everything else tells you it should have run out a long time ago.

wwwwwwww

Conversely, the sharp shears of pride and anger and judgment and selfishness will clip the long fuse of patience with amazing deftness. When I'm struggling to fit into the often-snug virtue of patience, it's helpful for me to ask myself if one of these vices is at play. When I think someone needs to just *get a hold of himself and pull it together already*, it's likely I'm reacting out of pride. Or when I'm harboring anger, patience means loosening my grip on that anger, which may not be an easy release.

Sometimes I find my impatience stemming from my self-righteous judgments; I want the clock to finally exclaim, *Time's up! Your mercy has just run out.* This may be because I'm judging through my own vantage point, not taking into account the person's hardships, history, or culture. And then I have those moments when I'm simply short with the people around me, because they're doing something like clanging dishes in the kitchen so I can't hear the television or accidentally treading on my neatly laid-out plans, all of which simmers down to basic selfishness.

Patience has a lot of enemies out there. It's like my cantankerous yard, where just about everything is out to get the grass. What is not out to trample our patience? But the virtue of patience is worth our preservation, because the patient person is truly one of the most beautiful reflections of God's character.

⋀⋀⋀⋀⋀⋀⋀⋀

My parents became this reflection when they invited my beloved and ailing grandparents on my mom's side to live with them. This was a tremendous adjustment on my parents' part, one I heavily championed from seven hundred miles away. I could hardly picture a more serene and nostalgic vignette than my parents and grandparents all nestled together under the same roof, sipping afternoon tea and planting tomatoes together by the back patio (my Southern pop knew how to grow a good "tomatuh"). I envisioned robust holidays with four generations communing by the fireplace, pacing ourselves over thick slices of pumpkin pie while snuggling with grandbabies and rooting for the Crimson Tide. These were some of my inflated ruminations that propelled me to do things like quote Isaiah 58:7 to my mom over the phone while she and my dad were praying about whether or not this was a good idea. To me it sounded just brilliant—*from Nashville*. Of course, I wasn't the one having to plan the dinner menus or mete out the medication. I didn't have to live with the squealing hearing aids. No doctor, library, or bank runs. Not an ounce of expended patience. Just billowy, warm feelings that sprang from my storybook ideas of extended family living together happily ever after.

My grandparents' move to my parents' house ended up being a shocking transition, especially for my mom, who was used to coming and going as she pleased at the autonomous age of fifty-five. Not to mention, if you've got history with anyone, you've probably got it with your parents, and having history is the one variable that can shoot patience to the moon. In most instances we can exhibit a long fuse with strangers, but when it comes to someone we know intimately, patience can expire like a firecracker. One stray comment, and *there it went.* My mom's patience was tugged upon by everything from the invasion of her privacy to having to answer a slew of questions throughout the day like, "Where'd the sugar-free cookies go?" or "Have you seen my biography of Princess Diana?"

This was not a sacrifice my parents could have made without the Holy Spirit breathing His life through them, without their understanding the great grace they themselves had been shown. I think if my parents had any virtue forged over those two years, it was their patience. It became transparently thin at times, stretched out like fine pizza dough, but it made for a lovely crust on which the other virtues could lie.

〜〜〜〜〜〜〜

It helps when I can actually tap into the understanding that God commands me to be patient because His very nature *is* patient. When we demonstrate this longsuffering, merciful, graceful characteristic, we are joyfully reminded that we grant such enduring patience to others because *patience* is who God is. I'm not trying to mimic Him so I can be a phenomenal Christian whom everyone can applaud or even to gain God's approval. I delight in demonstrating patience, because it proves God's character toward me. And because I am grateful to have received it, I am eager to extend it.

In 1 Timothy 1:15–16, Paul makes a bold statement about God's patience shown to him as an example to us: "Christ Jesus came into the world to save sinners—of whom I am the worst. But for that very reason I was shown mercy so that in me, the worst of sinners, Christ Jesus might display his *unlimited patience* as an example for those who would believe on him and receive eternal life." After a sweeping claim like this, it would be hard for anyone to think they had maxed-out God's patience, their sin somehow reaching beyond Paul's, who, according to him, had already secured first place in "the worst" category.

Paul wanted the unlimited patience of Christ in His life to be put on display, as though preserved behind spiritual glass and set in the museum of Scripture for thousands of years to come. You can hear his plea to us: *What I'm about to say is something you can trust, something you can fully accept. Jesus came to save sinners. And no one will ever outdo me here, because I was the worst of them. Yet Jesus showed me mercy. This act showcased His unlimited patience for all who would ever believe in Jesus and have unending life with Him.* Mercy and patience. We see the pairing here again.

〰〰〰〰〰〰

I have found patience to be a virtue more accurately shown than explained. This is why the gospels are so important when studying this quality, because Jesus shows it more than He explains it. One of the reasons I find patience difficult to nail down is because it's so closely intertwined with all the other virtues. I don't believe it can exist in a vacuum. You can't demonstrate patience without compassion, kindness, humility, gentleness, etc., which may be why Paul placed it last in his five-virtue run in Colossians. In a sense, patience doesn't mean anything unless it's in conjunction with all the others, because patience is the virtue that keeps the other ones going. It's the oil in the car of compassion. The yeast in the dough of kindness. And I can't imagine it being more entangled with forgiveness than it is.

My heart's desire is for more patience, mostly because it is a delicacy in a world of now, and split seconds, and *Don't slow me down.*

If our wardrobes are missing this article of patience, it is worth a slow stroll through the gospels, noting the ways in which Christ displayed His unlimited forbearance. It is worth an unhurried ramble through our own stories, journaling the patience that has been poured upon us, both by others and by Christ Himself. And lastly, it is worth the practice and sacrifice of intimately investing in the lives of the people around us, a commitment that is sure to refine our patience. As we seek the Holy Spirit for such strength and endurance, we know we will find Him, because it is His delight to clothe us in the character of Christ. Especially in patience, which keeps all the other ones working.

The Crowning Virtue

Joy

I was headed to the calming waters of the Chesapeake Bay in Maryland for a women's retreat during my college years. There's a formula to these retreats. You could mix it up a couple different ways, but the church beaker always held the same solution: late-night junk food, ridiculous skits performed by middle-aged women, small groups that fostered honest conversation, set in a town dotted with restaurants that proudly served up blue crab any way you could dream it. And when you were tranquilly full, you could roll out of your booth and into a string of antique shops that lined the streets. (I browsed only for the company—in college I barely had enough money for *new* things, much less double the money for old stuff.) And of course, the most potent ingredient of these late-winter retreats was the inspiring teaching. The speakers were always compelling.

The only issue I foresaw dampening this particular weekend was the topic. A few weeks before, I stood in the middle of the stairway of my parent's home, ripping open my mail and discovering that the retreat's theme was "How to Have True Joy." *Boo! Another message on something we all know is impossible.* This internal reaction teetered right on the line between my subconscious and conscious like an uncoordinated schoolboy trying to balance himself on a fence. He eventually fell on the side of my subconscious, so as not to be noticed but with a toe poking through the slats into my awareness. *Wait a minute.... Did I just think that?* Me talking back to myself: *Yes, you think joy is one of those things that makes for nice Christian messages and great Bible memory verses but is unattainable apart from fun and pleasure.* Myself responding to me: *Sigh.*

My own thinking had shocked me. Deep down I didn't think joy was possible unless you were a devout missionary who had somehow been divinely selected for it. And even if I could get at this joy, I wasn't sure I wanted it, because after all, joy seemed a little boring to me. Joy was the consolation prize for Christians who didn't—or weren't allowed to—have fun. The world got to have wild and crazy amusement; Christians got to have quiet, buttoned-up *joy.*

I have never forgotten my unruly disbelief in the reality of joy while standing on my parents' stairs, mostly because it caught me so off guard, naked as a Christian jaybird. There I stood with my retreat mail in hand, faithless at the prospect of anyone convincing me I could ever have deep and abiding joy apart from the highs and pleasures and entertainment found only in this world. So there you have it. Perhaps you understand my skepticism and thus plain disinterest in the matter.

ᴧᴧᴧᴧᴧᴧᴧᴧᴧᴧᴧᴧ

Though joy is not named in Colossians 3:12–17, the closely related practices of singing, praising, gratitude, and thanks are found in these verses. And since joy is talked about in so many other passages of Scripture, I wanted to address this hard-to-come-by quality, the one that people often say they have to *fight for!* I don't hear this grappling, struggling verb *fight* placed in front of any other virtue as much as I hear it preceding *joy.* And without pigeonholing any one culture, I find that the struggle for joy is much more present in affluent societies than anywhere else. At least this has been my observation. I think this is partially true because opulence and stuff and choices and comforts tend to complicate our lives, and joy is not complicated. Joy is simple and unencumbered. It doesn't need any of these things to exist, only God and the portions He gives.

This may sound pie-in-the-sky, but we find this to be true when we encounter people in poverty who have joy, because you don't need riches to possess joy. We hear about Christians in prisons and underground churches who are brimming with it, because you don't need physical freedom for joy to bubble up out of you. And there are those we've met, maybe even been close to, who are sick or dying but who have joy, because even health is not one of joy's prerequisites. Paul says in 2 Corinthians 7:4, "In all our troubles my joy knows no bounds." Paul could write this in earnest, because joy doesn't need our usual pleasures to exist. It can exist with our pleasures, but it doesn't rely on them to live or to thrive.

If we look at the gospels and epistles, we see that joy is tied to encounters with Jesus, to His message, and to His works. It came riding in on the tongues of angels when they heralded the birth of Christ. We see joy blossoming from the believers' fellowship, the spread of the gospel, and the growth of the church. We find it tethered to God's blessings. It is the crown of obedience. The word *joy* is sprinkled all over the New Testament, not as something topping the cupcakes of worldly lusts or entertainment but falling upon the hearts of men and women whose lives are caught up in who God is and what He is doing.

I think many of us miss out on the joy that springs from these wells because little of our lives revolve around these sources. We tend to look for joy in our next meal or in the compounding interest of our investments we gleefully watch grow. If we have a vacation on the books, we have joy. If the promotion happens, the dress fits, the boy calls, well then … *joy!* We look for little pockets of happiness to sustain us like quarters being popped into our joy meters—which are always ticking, always gobbling up whatever we just fed them. But true joy—the joy that Christ gives—is not like this. It doesn't burn up with use. When Christ gives joy, He gives it in fullness (John 15:11). We're freed from having to constantly feed the meter with our next big plan, pleasure, or purchase. Christ is our eternal measure.

ᴡᴡᴡᴡᴡᴡ

A few years ago the Lord took me out of a long and tumultuous time of struggle and sadness. When He finally pulled the curtain shut on that toilsome season, He reopened it upon a distinctly new act of emotional rest, successes, and solid friendships. My struggling-artist years had finally ended (at least for the time), the coins in my bank account could be measured in actual dollars, and as a rule, I had peace. My two feet had happily found solid ground, and I jumped and tumbled and twirled on this soil for joy that it was finally here.

The trouble with this dramatic change was that after I had gotten used to the ease and abundance—after the old struggles were but memories—I misplaced my joy. I found myself in an odd scenario where I had everything I enjoyed, yet I was strangely without joy. I couldn't figure out what was wrong with me. I had all my surefire delights at my bidding; how could I be so ungrateful and discontent?

The answer unfolded for me over time, and in its most distilled form I realized that I was missing an intimacy with God that had been vibrant in my previous years of excruciating loss and struggle. I'd had unexplainable joy in those hardships because I'd had unusual intimacy with Christ. It's why David could say "You have filled my heart with greater joy than when their grain and new wine abound" (Ps. 4:7). I was mistakenly looking for joy in the breadbaskets and glimmering decanters of my newly found ease and abundance, forgetting that joy is found in Christ's presence.

I had desperately wanted out of my anguish but never intended to wiggle out of my joy. I didn't want to go back to the way things were, but I missed sharing my tears with the Lord and having Him dab them with a verse or a timely answer. I longed for the

fellowship that only accompanies sharing in His sufferings, though
I was quick to point out that I didn't miss the sufferings part—just
that unmistakable *knowing* Him in them. Like the Lord spoke in
Isaiah, He had given me the treasures of darkness, the riches stored
in the secret places. These let me know that I was His and called by
name. And even during some agonizing moments, this gave me joy.

That I could revel in His gifts and deliverance while still clinging
to Him with love and pursuit was something that took a little time
for me to figure out. Yes, my joy would look a little different, because
a special portion of God's favor rests on the suffering, and I was no
longer suffering. But Christ-centered joy should never have to suffer
at the hands of wealth or ease. I realized that it was possible to still
experience the flame of its slow wick burning in my heart, even if the
ways I was desperate for Jesus took on a different form.

Part of this discovery required some retooling of my daily
routine and the way I was living my commission as a Christian. I
had to start planning for joy and putting myself in its path. Like a
good fisherman, I had to know where the honey holes were, where
joy bit most often. I knew from experience that my greatest joys
swirled around the presence and movement of Christ in my everyday reality. Typically I'm not that big of a crier, but put me in
front of a baptism or the testimony of a person whose life has been
lock, stock, and barrel resurrected by Jesus, and I'm a quivering-
mouthed, bleary-eyed wreck. Drop me in the jungles of Brazil and
let me see the transcendent smile of a man who used to worship
little wooden trinkets and practice witchcraft but whose chin now
tilts toward the sky because he knows Jesus, and suddenly I've got
a thrill I can't get at the theater.

I became intentional about pursuing joy by putting myself in position for it. I did really simple things like digging a little deeper into my church community. I kept an eye out for the straggler who might enjoy being at a dinner party I was throwing. When I sensed God nudging me, I pushed out of myself and sat with someone who needed advice over coffee, or I gave a little more money away. I started praying with a group of friends one morning a week. I made subtle changes with my time and resources out of obedience, but also because I knew in turn it would bring me the joy I had been missing.

wwwwwwww

I made a slightly more complicated move when I volunteered to teach that Bible study for women who have just gotten out of prison and who are addicted to things like substances and sex. I didn't have a clear idea of what I was getting into. I just knew that God wanted me to step out of my routine familiarity and become part of what He was doing in the lives of women so covered up from abuse and drugs they could hardly see straight, much less read their Bibles. At first I had to remind myself that these women didn't hate me, some of them just didn't have anything left for me, not even a smile that I was hoping they would feign so we could all pretend this whole thing was working.

With each passing week we peeled away a new layer of mistrust as we got to know one another and shared in the hopeful truths of Scripture. The ones that let us all know that Jesus has a special penchant for transforming the lives of abused, sinful, and utterly hopeless women. These seeds of truth were pressed into the soil of each one of their hearts, some still hiding dormant but some sprouting into glorious blooms none of us could have imagined. I watched one woman cry streaks of tears over an unabashed smile at the news of Christ's forgiveness. She had never known His act on the cross was *for her*. Now when she texts me, she always signs her messages, "Peace of mind." When I asked her why she signs her texts that way, she returned, "Because when you know Jesus, He gives you peace of mind." And then of course she signed it "Peace of mind." And, yes, this brought me joy.

The stuff that leads up to the baptisms, the moving testimonies, the chief burning his false gods in a blazing fire along the Amazon, and my friend ending her texts "Peace of mind" when before her mind was deafening chaos doesn't happen overnight. There's toiling and prayer and patience involved. There are late-night phone calls and discouraging setbacks. And sacrifices. There are dry spells when contending for joy. It makes me think of Hebrews 12:2: "Let us fix our eyes on Jesus … who for the *joy set before Him* endured the cross, scorning its shame, and sat down at the right hand of the throne of God." The prize was joy, but the path getting there was harrowing.

None of us will have the path that Christ had, but the principle is that sometimes there's a cost to joy, a bit of a journey along the way. Most of us experience more paltry inconveniences for the sake of joy, like when a limb starts to fall asleep during a prayer meeting or when we can tell we're going to miss the last quarter of the football game because it's our night to work in the nursery. Sometimes my friends and I have to talk ourselves up on the way to things like Bible study or service projects, we have to grab one another by the collar and coax one another into the car. But almost every time, we leave with joy, and on the ride home we're happy that we aimed for joy instead of something easier but not nearly so rich.

.ᴧᴧᴧᴧᴧᴧᴧᴧᴧᴧᴧᴧᴧ.

> Just as the Father has loved Me, I have also loved you; abide in My love. If you keep My commandments, you will abide in My love; just as I have kept My Father's commandments and abide in His love. These things I have spoken to you so that My joy may be in you, and that *your joy may be made full.* (John 15:9–11 NASB)

Trying to clothe ourselves in the virtues outside of the fitting room of being chosen, holy, and loved will prove a maddening endeavor of dress-up. We may look the part in the moment, but inevitably the tight collars of moralism and crooked hems of behavior management will eventually give us away. There is no need for such striving when words like "I have also loved you" have already been spoken. It's this love of Christ that lets us out of the suffocating garments of do-goodism for approval, giving us the grace to obey God's commands while we revel in His affection. Keeping His commands is not grievous; it's a delightful expression of our love for God, because He has first loved us (1 John 4:19; 5:3).

And so we abide in this love by taking off the old and putting on the new. We fulfill it by offering the cup of forgiveness and exchanging our bitterness for grace. By choosing the peace of Christ as the rule of our hearts and toiling for it in our relationships. We abide in His love when we extend the hand of kindness and bow with the heart of humility. When we let the marching crowd pass us for the sake of compassion, and when we invite patience to respond in place of short fuses and frustration.

As we abide in His love, and thus fulfill His commands, we will discover a prize that soars past the peaks of earthly pleasures, a crown more enduring than happiness. *Joy.* Jesus has come that we may have it *to the full.*

Discussion Questions

(Editor's note: Because chapter 1 is an introduction to the virtues, we have started this section with chapter 2, "Pick Me, Pick Me.")

Chapter 2: Pick Me, Pick Me

1. Have someone in your group read Colossians 3:12. How do you think knowing that God chooses you is meant to help you live out the virtues?

2. Do you feel confident in God's special choosing of you, or is this a truth you struggle with? Explain.

3. Share about a relationship in which you feel particularly chosen. Describe the benefits and blessings of knowing that someone chooses you.

4. Verses from Psalm 139 are mentioned in this chapter. What elements from Psalm 139 assure you of God's distinctive delight in choosing you?

5. How does knowing that you are chosen by God free you to live the virtues you find the most challenging?

Chapter 3: Pointy Sticks and Behavior Management

1. What kind of religious environment did you grow up in (if any)? Was holiness something you tried to earn? Something you understood you could grow in by the grace of Christ? Something you knew nothing about?

2. Have you ever been burdened by legalism? If so, how does the gift of being made holy differ from trying to manage your behavior in your own strength?

3. If you feel comfortable, is there something you can share with the group that consistently keeps you from feeling holy in God's sight? How does the truth of justification challenge the guilt and shame that hinders us from walking in holiness?

4. How does the idea of being set apart shape the way you live (if at all)?

5. Wayne Grudem is quoted in this chapter as saying, "Justification is an instantaneous legal act of God in which he (1) thinks of

our sins as forgiven and Christ's righteousness as belonging to us, and (2) declares us to be righteous in his sight." How does this understanding free you to live the virtues you find the most challenging?

Chapter 4: Father Loves You

1. In Colossians 3:12, the apostle Paul addresses believers as chosen, holy, and dearly loved. How does being dearly loved by God affect the way you view your call to live virtuously?

2. Do you struggle with accepting God's unfathomable love for you? Why or why not? How does your acceptance of God's love affect the way you live out virtues like patience, forgiveness, peace, kindness, joy, etc.?

3. Do you know someone who deeply revels in God's love for him or her? Describe the qualities of this person.

4. Do you feel less loved or lovable when you're aware that you lack some virtue? If so, explain.

5. Share with the group a passage of Scripture that speaks to your heart about the love of God.

6. What are the biggest hindrances in your life to accepting and reveling in God's love? How can you effectively deal with these hindrances?

Chapter 5: The Angel in the Stone

1. How does the concept of a sculptor creating by taking away help you when looking at Colossians 2:11?

2. Like the excess stone that the sculptor chips away, what hindrances or sins need to be chipped away from your life so that you can more fully express the virtues?

3. What "old" patterns in your life challenge your ability to live the virtues? How can you rid your life of these practices and habits?

4. How do you go about putting to death the habits of your old self? What does this involve other than working really, really hard to be good?

5. When you are aware of a negative habit in yourself—such as excess anger, deceitfulness, or an evil desire—what goes on between you and God in your prayer time? For instance, do you confess the sin? Do you express frustration at yourself or God? Do you thank God for revealing what's in your heart and welcome more exposure? Do you talk with Him about what might be fueling this habit? Do you avoid prayer altogether at those times?

Chapter 6: The Perfect Storm

1. After reading this chapter, are you aware of any unforgiveness you are harboring in your heart? Without betraying or exposing anyone, can you share about this struggle to forgive? (Maybe you can name the

harm: betrayal; a lie told about you; sexual assault; infidelity; hurtful words said in anger. Perhaps also name your feelings: anger, sadness, humiliation, loss, fear.)

2. Complete this sentence: "If I let go of the demand that this person pay for what they did, then _____."

3. The deeper our grasp of Jesus' forgiveness for us, the greater our ability to forgive. In practical terms, how can you reflect on the forgiveness that Jesus has shown you? In what ways does this help you in forgiving others?

4. Can you share a story about the freedom, relief, and healing that came as a result of your forgiving someone? (Again, without exposing anyone.)

5. Does forgiveness mean trusting the other person to get close to you again? Explain.

6. How does Luke 7:36–50 help you grasp your need for God's mercy and forgiveness? Do you think you've accepted God's forgiveness on an intellectual level but not on a heart level? If so, how can you personally internalize His incredible forgiveness?

Chapter 7: Yes, You Really Can

1. In what ways do you see forgiveness and peace being closely related? In the same way, how do you see bitterness and unrest as being intimately tied together?

2. What misconceptions about forgiveness have kept you from forgiving? (For instance, thinking that forgiving means the person's wrongdoing wasn't really wrong.)

3. How has unforgiveness in your life been tied to your desire to maintain control?

4. First Peter 4:19 says that we should entrust ourselves to our faithful Creator, even in suffering. How does offering forgiveness to someone cause you to give up control to God? What practical comforts can you take away from entrusting yourself to your faithful Creator?

5. Is there any specific situation where you have given up on the hope of being able to forgive? If so, explain.

6. How does the story of Joseph affect you with regard to forgiveness? For example, does it inspire you that forgiveness is always possible by the grace of God, even for the situation you named in question 5?

Chapter 8: Not as the World Gives

1. What are some of the obstacles to peace in your life?

2. In what ways do you struggle with having peace with God? (For example, unbelief, lack of faith or trust, disappointment with Him.) How does your lack of peace with God affect your peace with others?

3. What fears disrupt your peace? In what ways are you learning to trust God with those fears, therefore restoring an inner peace in your life?

4. Do you carry around guilt and shame that regularly disrupt your peace with God? How can you practically trust Romans 5:1, which says, "Therefore, since we have been justified through faith, we have *peace* with God through our Lord Jesus Christ."

5. The world offers many paper-thin comforts that give us a false sense of peace. In what specific ways have you run to those "comforts"? Conversely, in what ways have you experienced the true peace that Jesus offers? How do the two differ?

Chapter 9: A Soul at Rest

1. In what ways have you forfeited your own peace through disobedience?

2. On the other hand, describe the connections you've experienced between obedience and peace.

3. Discuss the story of Jonah and the way in which he sacrificed peace for the illusion of being in control. How can you relate?

4. Share about a time when repentance restored your inner peace.

5. Give an example of a time when you had deep, abiding peace when everything around you was anything but calm. What made the difference?

Chapter 10: And Then Came the Rains
1. How is kindness powerful? After reading this chapter, in what ways do you more deeply value the virtue of kindness?

2. In what practical ways can you demonstrate kindness to the people around you, whether strangers or intimate family members and friends?

3. What challenges your spirit of kindness the most? (Think of things outside you, such as rude people, selfish family members, or proud coworkers. Think also of things inside you, such as fear, busyness, or worrying about whether your own needs are being met.)

4. How can you distinguish between the true kindness that is fueled by the Holy Spirit and having a regularly nice disposition?

5. Describe a time when someone showed you lavish kindness that you weren't expecting or didn't deserve. How did it affect or change you?

Chapter 11: Everything Must Die (To Rise Again)

1. Our society tends to push the idea of looking out for ourselves and promoting our successes. How does this rival the Christian call for us to live lives of humility?

2. Share about a time when God took you through a season of humbling. What were the results? Did you experience any new life growing from that time?

3. Look at Philippians 2:5–11. What do you find to be the most difficult part of this passage? What do you see as the most promising?

4. Where are the hardest places for you to show humility? (For example, within your home, at your workplace, while around a particular individual, while competing in sports?) What about these particular situations challenges your pride? How can you practically lay your pride down before the Lord so that humility, and therefore freedom, can follow?

5. Scripture is clear that Jesus exalts the humble. How does this encourage you as you seek to live in the posture of humility?

Chapter 12: When the Crowds Keep Marching

1. This chapter talks about the connection between humility and compassion. Have you ever thought of this before? If so, describe how humbling experiences in your own life have caused you to be more compassionate. (Conversely, how has your pride kept you from being compassionate?)

2. Luke 18:35–43 talks about an uncompassionate crowd and God's patient mercy toward a blind beggar. What did you learn from this passage? What surprised or moved you?

3. What challenges your compassion the most? (For example, people who don't seem to appreciate or deserve it.) How can reflecting on God's compassion for you directly affect your compassion for others?

4. Do you have a hard time breaking from your busy plans to show someone compassion? How can you practically extend compassion in the midst of busyness?

5. Share a story about a time when you've seen the dramatic results of showing or being shown compassion. Perhaps you've experienced this on a missions trip, through someone at your church, or within your own family.

Chapter 13: More Than a Disposition

1. What tries your patience the most? After giving some specific examples, why do you think these things particularly challenge your patience?

2. Share about a time when God showed you incredible patience. This will be most helpful if you share specifically. Describe what this did to your relationship with Him. (If you can't think of a time when God was patient with you, what does this say about the way you view God?)

3. How has a strong grasp on God's patience with you helped you in showing patience with others? Or how has a sense that you haven't needed or received God's patience affected the way you treat others?

4. What's the relationship between patience and mercy? In what ways are you lacking in mercy, and therefore in patience?

5. Describe a season in your life when God taught you patience in new measures. Try to focus on an actual period in your life, as opposed to a specific situation. What did you learn? How did you change?

Chapter 14: The Crowning Virtue
1. Have you given up hope on having true joy in your life—joy that is not necessarily attached to earthly pleasures? If so, why?

2. What is joy like for a person who doesn't naturally have an enthusiastic or emotional temperament?

3. Can you recall a time in your life when God gave you true joy in the midst of trying circumstances? If so, describe this supernatural joy if you can put words to it.

4. What tends to rob you of your joy? How can you combat these thieves with the truths of Scripture?

5. Colossians 3:15–17 talks about giving thanks, praising, encouraging, and singing with one another. How can practicing these things increase your joy?

6. Share about a person who is incredibly joyful in the Lord. What does joy look like in his or her life? What do you admire the most about him or her?

7. What will you take away from this book about the virtues?

Notes

Chapter 3: Pointy Sticks and Behavior Management

1. Wayne Grudem, *Systematic Theology* (Grand Rapids, MI: Zondervan, 2000), 723.

2. As quoted in William R. Moody, *The Life of Dwight L. Moody* (Chicago: Fleming H. Revell, 1900), 368.

Chapter 4: Father Loves You

1. ἀγαπάω (*agapao*), Joseph Henry Thayer, *A Greek-English Lexicon of the New Testament* (public domain, 1889), Blue Letter Bible, www.blueletterbible.org/lang/lexicon/lexicon.cfm?Strongs=G25&t=KJV (accessed October 22, 2010).

Chapter 5: The Angel in the Stone

1. Warren W. Wiersbe, *The Wiersbe Bible Commentary: New Testament* (Colorado Springs, CO: David C Cook, 2007), 678.

2. Dallas Willard, *The Great Omission* (New York: HarperOne, 2006), 133.

Chapter 7: Yes, You Really Can

1. C. S. Lewis, *Mere Christianity* (New York: HarperCollins, 2001), 117.

Chapter 8: Not as the World Gives

1. Francis Brown, S. R. Driver, and C. A. Briggs, *A Hebrew and English Lexicon of the Old Testament* (Oxford: Oxford University Press, 1952), available at www.eliyah. com/lexicon.html (accessed July 27, 2010).

2. Elizabeth Gilbert, *Eat, Pray, Love* (New York: Viking Penguin, 2006), 14.

3. John Stott, *Christian Mission in the Modern World* (Downers Grove, IL: InterVarsity, 1975), 50.

4. Charles H. Spurgeon, "The Best of Masters," sermon number 247, April 10, 1859, The Spurgeon Archive, www.spurgeon.org/sermons/0247.htm (accessed October 25, 2010).

Chapter 9: A Soul at Rest

1. Dietrich Bonhoeffer, *The Cost of Discipleship* (New York: Touchstone, 1995), 178.

Chapter 10: And Then Came the Rains

1. St. Augustine, *Confessions,* trans. J. G. Pilkington (Edinburgh, United Kingdom: T. & T. Clark, 1876), 104.

Chapter 11: Everything Must Die (To Rise Again)

1. "On the Third Day" by Matt Maher and Marc Byrd © 2006 ThankYou Music.

2. J. Oswald Sanders, *A Spiritual Clinic* (Chicago: Moody, 1958), 23.

3. Ibid., 25.

Chapter 13: More Than a Disposition

1. Spiros Zodhiates, *The Complete Word Study Dictionary: New Testament* (Chattanooga, TN: AMG, 1992), 1425.

2. Beth Moore, *Living Beyond Yourself: Exploring the Fruit of the Spirit* (Nashville, TN: Lifeway, 1998), 119.